TELEVISION PRODUCTION
for
Elementary and Middle Schools

Also by Keith Kyker and Christopher Curchy

Television Production: A Classroom Approach

Instructor Edition (includes Book 1 and Book 2 below). 1993.
Student Edition, Book 1 (Beginning). 1993
Student Edition, Book 2 (Advanced). 1993
Video (75 minutes).

A complete curriculum package, classroom tested and filled with helpful diagrams and photographs that offers students in grades 7-12 a hands-on approach to learning all aspects of television production.

The above titles and video can be ordered from:

Libraries Unlimited, Inc.
P.O. Box 6633
Englewood, CO 80155-6633

1-800-237-6124

TELEVISION PRODUCTION
for
Elementary and Middle Schools

Keith Kyker
and
Christopher Curchy

Illustrated by Mike Lalone
Photography by Gaylen Berlinger and Keith Kyker
Graphics by Eric Picardi and Mark Volpe

1994
Libraries Unlimited, Inc.
Englewood, Colorado

For my mother and father, who made sure that I was clothed, well-fed, and knew the value of education. My life is fulfilling because of your groundwork.

— K. K.

For my friend, Bill Corrente, who helped me make my first elementary news show.

— C. C.

LIBRARIES UNLIMITED, INC.
P.O. Box 6633
Englewood, CO 80155-6633
1-800-237-6124

Project Editor: Stephen Haenel
Copy Editor: Jan Krygier
Proofreader: Ann Marie Damian
Design and Layout: Alan Livingston

Library of Congress Cataloging-in-Publication Data

Cataloging for first printing:

Kyker, Keith.
  Television production for elementary schools / Keith Kyker and
Christopher Curchy ; illus. by Mike Lalone ; photography by Gaylen
Berlinger and Keith Kyker ; graphics by Eric Picardi and Mark Volpe.
  xiv, 211 p. 22x28 cm.
  Includes bibliographical references and index.
  ISBN 1-56308-186-5
  1. Television in elementary education--United States. 2. Television
--United States--Production and direction. I. Curchy, Christopher.
II. Title.
LB1044.7.K95 1994   94-10906
371.3'356--dc20   CIP

CONTENTS

Part II
STUDENT CURRICULUM

ACKNOWLEDGMENTS

The authors would like to thank the following individuals and groups for their contributions to this work:

The administration and staff at WCPX Channel 6, Orlando, Florida, including

Sandy Bengston, Public Relations
Willy Doby, Director
Ashley Udell, Producer
Mary Hamill, News Anchor
Pat Michaels, Weather Anchor
Kathy Yarosh, Writer/Producer
Chris Flora, Audio Engineer
Dave Treiber, Videographer/Editor
Julie Northlake, Electronic Graphic Artist

Pro Video and Computer Depot, Inc., of Orlando, Florida

Shirley Pettit, Program Consultant, Library Media Services, Orange County Public Schools, Florida

Shure Brothers, Inc., Evanston, Illinois

Panasonic Professional/Industrial Video, Secaucus, New Jersey

Videonics, Campbell, California

Dr. Stan Kmet, Florida Institute for Film Education

Dr. David Loertscher, Debby Mattil, and the entire helpful staff of Libraries Unlimited, Inc., Englewood, Colorado

Dr. Donna Baumbach, University of Central Florida, Orlando, Florida

INTRODUCTION

Since the publication of our first book, *Television Production: A Classroom Approach*, we have had the opportunity to meet many media specialists and teachers who work with television production in schools. We expected that. What we didn't expect was that so many of them would be working in elementary and middle schools. At media conferences and school speaking engagements, at least half of the participants are elementary and middle school media specialists and teachers, working with television production on a daily basis. They are producing news shows, creating orientation tapes, and videotaping guest speakers. In short, they are providing a valuable service to their schools.

So, quite naturally, we decided to provide a resource book for media specialists and teachers that explains and clarifies the field of television production, and makes some concrete recommendations for use of the medium in elementary and middle school settings. After talking with several of these dedicated educators, we developed a working table of contents that has undergone at least a dozen rewrites. We think we've finally got the formula for a book designed to help, explain, and motivate. In other words, we hope this book makes your job just a little bit easier.

Chapter 1, "Operating a Television Production System," provides a detailed explanation of the function and operation of television production equipment—everything from the basic camcorder to switchers, audio mixers, and character generators. The chapter also features tips on picture composition and equipment security.

Chapter 2 explores "News Show Creation and Content" in the elementary and middle school. Do you pledge allegiance to the flag, read the lunch menu, and then sign off? This chapter will give you helpful information on news show content, as well as establishing guidelines and philosophies for your programs, creating interesting segments, and building a student news team.

Chapter 3 offers no-nonsense guidelines for providing videotape services for your school. Most media specialists and teachers have been asked, at one time or another, to videotape guest speakers, class sessions, and assembly programs. "Videotape Services for Your School" shows you the painless way to achieve professional results.

Chapter 4, "Using Video to Teach Media Skills," offers grade-specific activities using video to teach students how to use the school library media center. Designed to stimulate interest in the media center, these activities should add a special magic to "library time."

Chapter 5 walks you through the step-by-step process of "Producing Videotape Programs for Your School." Using the example of a school orientation tape, the chapter details shooting practices, as well as pre- and postproduction activities essential to your program's success.

Chapter 6 explores an area about which most of us need to learn a little bit more: "School-Vendor Relationships." Most television production teachers will need to buy new equipment from time to time. How can we be sure we're getting a good deal? What questions should we ask? At what point is price *not* the most important issue? Reading this chapter should give you much more confidence when making your equipment and blank videotape purchases.

We wouldn't omit one of the most popular features of our first book, "Questions from the Floor." Chapter 7 answers the most frequently asked questions with a decidedly elementary and middle school school slant.

Let's face it—the material described above would stand alone as a valuable resource. But we like TV so much that we decided to throw in something for the "kiddies"! The second half of this book features 20 student lessons that describe some of the basic concepts of television production and news gathering. These teaching lessons feature easy-to-read text, helpful illustrations, student questions and activities, and teacher advisories. The first student section, student lessons, features nine lessons that focus on particular aspects of television production. The second student section, "Careers in Television," spotlights the duties, education, and experiences of eight real-life television professionals working for a major-market CBS affiliate. Finally, four of the basic physical science concepts of television production are explained in object lesson plans that establish *you* as the expert.

Of course, all of the student lesson pages for your students may be photocopied. Students can even make their own television production notebooks. Imagine the gratitude on your colleagues' faces when you provide them with a month's worth of enrichment activities that will stimulate *and* educate.

We can't imagine a book like this without a complete glossary. We've selected more than 100 terms from the text and defined them in practical, experience-related terms. The comprehensive index will help you review those important concepts or find quick answers to those tough questions like "Why does a microphone work?"

Which leads to more conversations. To paraphrase one of our former instructional technology professors, "High-tech *and* high-touch." That's where you come in. Our hope is that this book makes the humanizing of technology that much easier in the elementary and middle school settings.

Enjoy.

Part I
TELEVISION
PRODUCTION

1 OPERATING A TELEVISION PRODUCTION SYSTEM

Basic Television Production Equipment

Teachers and media specialists have varying levels of knowledge about television production equipment. Some will have college training or personal experience with video production as a hobby. Others will have little or no knowledge and be apprehensive about even holding the equipment. Most teachers and media specialists will fall somewhere in between.

This chapter presents an overview of production equipment. The chapters that follow will assume most of the knowledge presented here. Wherever you fit in the descriptions above, you can probably learn something from the pages that follow. This chapter will also serve as a good introduction to the technology of television production.

Modern technology has made operating video production equipment quite simple. Most equipment manufacturers take pride making products that are easy to learn and operate. However, making full use of this equipment in an educational setting requires an understanding of the equipment and the features each item offers.

The Camcorder

The camcorder (fig. 1.1 on page 4) is the most obvious and recognized item of television production equipment found in elementary and middle schools. In fact, almost every school has one or more camcorders for the faculty and students to use.

As you've probably figured out, the word *camcorder* is a combination of the words *camera* and *recorder*. When portable video equipment became available and affordable to most elementary and secondary schools (in the early 1980s), the systems consisted of two pieces—the video camera and the videocassette recorder (VCR). Together, these items were quite large and bulky by today's standards. Few adults and even fewer students could be expected to carry and operate both a video camera and a videotape recorder. Videography was a task performed by a two-person team or a single camera operator with a VCR on a media cart. Aside from the obvious disadvantages, the video camera and VCR had to be connected with a length of video cable. This may seem to be a minor concern, but these cables, often connected permanently to the video camera, could become disconnected during production or broken by an errant footstep or a media cart wheel. When technology allowed video equipment to become much smaller, the permanent connection of the video camera and videocassette recorder was a natural choice.

Today, camcorders offer excellent quality at a very reasonable price. Picture quality that formerly could only be obtained by rooms full of video equipment can now be produced with a camcorder that rests comfortably on the shoulder. Once the realm of the hobbyist, the camcorder is now the most familiar format for portable television production. Even television stations use professional camcorders for gathering news outside of the studio.

Fig. 1.1. Camcorder. Photo courtesy of Panasonic.

How the Camcorder Works

Now that you're thinking about the video camera and VCR as one piece of equipment, reverse your thinking! In order to understand how the camcorder works, it is best to consider the two parts of the camcorder individually. A simple way to understand the function of the equipment is to remember that a video camera converts light into an electrical signal and the videocassette recorder stores that signal on a magnetic tape. The VCR also reads the magnetic tape and sends the signal to a television set for viewing. It may help at this point to grab a camcorder off the shelf and determine just where the video camera ends and the VCR begins. You may be surprised at just how little room the video camera takes.

The Video Camera. To understand how a video camera works, we really only need to learn about three parts of the camera: the lens, the imaging device, and the viewfinder.

The *lens* is a curved glass that collects light from the physical environment and produces a small image. The curvature of the lens allows light to be gathered from a wide vista. As you've probably noticed from observing professional still-camera photographers, lenses come in a variety of sizes. The most diverse characteristic of these lenses is their length. In fact, lenses are usually described using terms that refer to their length, called focal length. The focal length is the measurement, usually expressed in millimeters, from the optical center of the lens to the front of the imaging device (which we'll explain later). A very long lens is called a telephoto lens. A telephoto lens can provide a close-up from a great distance. Telephoto lenses are used extensively in sports. The photographer who gets a close-up of the batter from beyond the center field fence is using a telephoto lens. The opposite of the long telephoto lens is the wide-angle lens. As you've probably guessed, the wide-angle lens is used for wide shots of groups. Unlike the telephoto lens, the wide-angle lens is quite short and flat. If a photographer is taking a picture of a group or class, he or she is probably using a wide-angle lens.

Although telephoto and wide-angle lenses allow photos to be taken at extremes of distance, they are not without disadvantages. The telephoto lens has the tendency to compress space. People or objects photographed with a telephoto lens appear to be standing very close together, even if they are many feet apart. Reconsider our photograph taken from center field. In our photograph of the home plate area, we may see the umpire, the catcher, the batter, the pitcher, and a runner on second base. All of these players will appear to be standing next to one another, even though the batter is more than 100 feet from the runner on second base. The wide-angle lens can produce barrel distortion. People standing on the ends of rows in a club photograph can appear to be "leaning in," as their bodies curve toward the middle. This is also known as a "fish-eye" effect. Great care must be taken when using telephoto and wide-angle lenses.

At this point you're probably wondering two things: (1) Why does my camcorder only have one permanently attached lens? and (2) Why all the talk about still cameras? Let's let the second question answer the first one. Serious photographers may own several very good lenses, from which they select the one that best serves their given needs, and attach it to the camera body. You have probably seen a professional photographer grab a lens from his or her pocketed vest and quickly attach it to a camera body. For several reasons, the most obvious being the "moving" nature of video, this is not practical for the videographer. Therefore, most video cameras and camcorders are equipped with a single, multipurpose lens, called a zoom lens. A zoom lens is actually a lens within a lens. On the outside, the zoom lens appears to be a medium-sized lens. But inside the zoom lens is another lens that further shapes the light entering the camera. That lens is usually pulled forward and backward on a small track inside the lens housing. If you have a camcorder handy, try looking into the lens while you zoom in and out. You should see the third lens moving within the housing. When you moved the zoom lens, you probably operated a small motor mounted beside the lens housing. The buttons that are pushed to operate this lens are usually labeled "T" and "W" for, you guessed it, telephoto and wide-angle. By pushing the "telephoto" button, you can move the internal lens away from the camera body. Pushing the "wide-angle" button moves the internal lens back toward the camera body, creating a shorter focal length.

The numbers on the side of the zoom lens indicate the range of the zoom lens. The number is called the zoom ratio, and is usually expressed with the "x" symbol (for example, 12 x 1) or the ":" symbol (12:1). The first number refers to the telephoto capability and the second number refers to the wide-angle ability. This ratio means that the lens can "see" 12 times normal vision. In other words, a 12 x 1 lens makes the subject appear 12 times larger. When the lens is zoomed-in all the way, the "1" represents normal vision. When the lens is zoomed-out to the wide-angle position, the view approximates normal vision. This lens is typical for camcorders, and should be strong enough to complete most video tasks. Some video cameras will have a 4 x 1 or 6 x 1 lens, which can severely limit your ability to get a close-up of a guest speaker from across a large classroom or auditorium.

The light gathered by the lens is converted into an electrical signal by the *imaging device*. Two types of imaging devices are used in video cameras: the tube and the charge-coupled device (CCD; fig. 1.2). Early video cameras used tubes as imaging devices. The light from the lens is focused onto the front of the tube, which converts the light into electrical signals. The first tubes were about the size of a roll of paper towels. When widespread use of video tubes ended in the mid-1980s the tubes were about the size of a felt-tip marker. However, the size and fragile nature of video tubes led manufacturers to adopt the charge-coupled device as the standard imaging device in video cameras. CCDs, also called "chips," are about the size of a postage stamp. Video cameras can use a single chip to produce a quality video signal; professional cameras use up to three chips to process the picture. The CCD, or chip, is

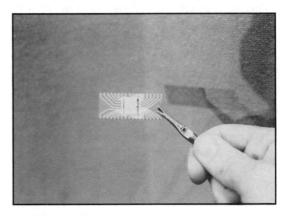

Fig. 1.2. CCD.

actually a photosensitive material that converts light into an electrical signal. In other words, the light that comes from the lens is focused onto the front of the CCD. The CCD then converts that light into an electrical signal. The CCD surface (about ½ inch across) is divided into several thousand light-sensing areas called "pixels." Each pixel is capable of detecting the presence of light. The quality of the video picture is largely determined by the number of pixels on the CCD. Imagine that you have been commissioned to create a large mural using mosaic tile. You have an unlimited amount of time to complete the mural, and your pay will be determined by the sharpness and clarity of your mural. Would you prefer thousands of small tiles, or a few very large tiles? Obviously, the small tiles would give you a sharper image. The same principle holds true with CCD size and the number of pixels.

The *viewfinder* is the small television mounted on the camera that allows the videographer to see what he or she is videotaping. Most viewfinders are monochrome (black and white), but some color viewfinders are available. Color viewfinders offer no real advantage over monochrome versions. Monochrome video is generally crisper and sharper, and therefore better for the small viewfinder. Camcorder viewfinders are often capable of providing valuable information for the videographer. Messages inside the viewfinder may include a battery power monitor, a tape counter, a record indicator, and the white balance setting. These features and their symbols can vary greatly by manufacturer. Consult your owner's manual to gain a full understanding of the features of your camcorder's viewfinder.

The lens, imaging device, and viewfinder all work together to allow light-to-electricity conversion. The lens gathers the light that the imaging device converts into electricity. The viewfinder allows the videographer to see the picture processed by the camera.

The Videocassette Recorder. The signal created by the video camera can be recorded by the videocassette recorder. The VCR consists of a series of two or four magnetic tape heads, a motorized mechanism that pulls the videotape past the heads, and a series of control buttons that tells the head assembly and mechanism how to function.

A VCR head is a magnet that places a small electrical charge onto the videotape. Videotape is actually a plastic base onto which a thin coating of metallic particles has been glued. Those magnetic charges are stored onto the videotape. The VCR can interpret those charges in the playback mode and convert the charges into a signal used by a television set. The VCR heads are actually mounted on a drum that spins very quickly inside the VCR. This enables the heads to record a great deal of information on the tape in a short period of time.

On a two-head VCR, one head handles all of the record and playback functions (both audio and video) and the second head serves simply as a magnet that erases the tape before it is recorded. A four-head VCR has (1) an erase head, (2) a video record/playback head, (3) an audio record/playback head, often divided in half for stereo recording, and (4) a "flying" head that kicks in when the VCR is on "pause" or "still," allowing for a clear still image on pause and glitch-free recording when pausing. Most camcorders are equipped with four-head VCRs to eliminate excessive static/snow (video noise) between recorded segments.

Video heads are very small; they are measured in microns. A micron is one millionth of a meter. For this reason, great care should be taken with the internal workings of the VCR. One mite of dirt can smear onto the VCR head, making it unusable. Many technicians keep a dust cloth beside each VCR in their studio to wipe the surface of videocassettes before each use. Be careful when applying stickers or labels to your videotape. If a label falls off into your VCR, it could mean big trouble for your video heads, not to mention an expensive repair bill. Video heads should be cleaned professionally periodically, depending on how much use the VCR gets during the school year. Your industrial video dealer can recommend a head-cleaning videocassette to use in between professional service. The VCR heads represent a substantial cost of the camcorder. Replacing them can cost more than $100. In video, an ounce of prevention is always worth a pound of cure.

The motorized mechanism of the VCR features two tape hubs that correspond to the hubs in the back of the videocassette, a capstan that pulls the tape past the tape heads, and a motor to provide the power. When a standard VHS videocassette is inserted into the VCR, the VCR pushes two buttons on the videocassette. These two buttons allow a small amount of tape to be pulled from the cassette and looped around the VCR's heads. The first button, located on the side, near the actual tape, allows a trap door to be opened on the top of the tape. The second button, on the back of the videotape, "unlocks" the videotape hubs and allows the tape to transfer from one spindle to the other within the cassette. The capstan is a small, motorized cylinder that pulls the tape past the VCR heads. The tape is usually pressed between the capstan and a rubber pinch wheel.

The VCR also contains several operational controls. Play, record, fast-forward, rewind, stop, and pause are all features familiar to just about everybody. The VCR part of the camcorder may include other controls, such as audio dub and video insert functions. Some camcorders even have a timer or animation function. Although it is best to consult the owner's manual for specific direction, a brief explanation of these controls is presented here. Audio dub means replacing the old audio already on a videotape with new audio. For example, let's say that you are creating a media center orientation tape. You have made several 10-second shots of the circulation desk, newspaper rack, magazine rack, stacks, etc., and you wish to add some simple narration. You can do this by connecting a microphone to the "mic" jack on the camcorder, or simply using the microphone already mounted on the camcorder. Then, by activating the audio dub button you can add your narration while you watch the video shots in the viewfinder. The VCR part of the camcorder is actually erasing the old audio while recording new audio (in this case, your narration). Video insert, found on many camcorders, is very similar, except that new video is inserted. This usually involves connecting another VCR or camcorder to your camcorder. Obviously, it is important to consult the owner's manual for an explanation of this operation.

Two controls that may pique the interest of students using the camcorder are the animation controls and the automatic timer. Placing your camcorder in the animation mode will allow you to create simple stop action animation projects. Usually, pushing the "trigger" start/stop button on a camcorder will roll the videotape until the button is pushed again to stop the recording. However, in the animation mode, each trigger push rolls tape for about one-fourth of a second. If the camera is set on a tripod for steadiness, the objects in the scene can be moved between shots. For example, imagine that you are creating a brief video program showing students where to put the books they are returning to the media center. You could make an animated "parade" of books marching across the circulation desk and diving into the slot marked "book return." To do this, simply establish your scene by putting the camera on a tripod in front of the circulation desk and activating the animation function as described in your owner's manual. Remember, each push of the trigger will record tape for about one-fourth of a second. Push the trigger about a dozen times to record three seconds of the stationary shot. Then move the books slightly toward the "book return" slot. Record one-fourth second by pressing the trigger. Then move the books again, and record another segment. Continue until all of the books have reached the slot. After a few minutes of work you will have a one-minute animation segment that will capture the attention of most of your students and get your point across. (This segment could be combined with shots of the media specialist saying "Alright books, let's get moving. Hup, two, three, four..." to make the segment more fun and memorable.) Students can also be very inventive with modeling clay and sand sculpturing using this simple animation technique.

The timer function found on many camcorders is similar to the animation function. The camcorder can be programmed to record a brief amount of videotape periodically. For example, you could automatically record one second of video every minute. To show the students, faculty, and administration just how busy the media center is, set a camcorder on a tripod in a corner of the center and activate the timer function. Leave the camcorder in the same place for about an hour. The result will be a one-minute program that shows the activity of the area for the last hour.

Camcorder Controls and Adjustments

Camcorders are quite convenient when you need to pop in a tape and immediately begin recording. However, there are some simple adjustments that should be made each time the camcorder is used, and there are some other features of the camcorder that may be worth knowing about when faced with a difficult shooting situation.

White Balance. The white balance of a video camera or camcorder determines how the camera processes color. When we walk into a room, we usually don't think of the light in the room as having a color, unless the dramatic effects of colored lights are present. However, the camcorder is unable to overcome slight variations in the color of light. Generally speaking, sunlight, candlelight, and the light from standard light bulbs has a reddish tint; fluorescent light has a bluish tint. The camcorder's white balance control makes minor adjustments in the color output of the camera, thereby correcting any color distortion. More professional camera/VCR systems have a manual white balance, which requires holding a piece of white paper in front of the camera and pushing a series of buttons. Most camcorders have simplified this process by installing a white filter in the camera, or providing an indoor/outdoor white balance choice. Whether white-balancing takes twenty seconds or two seconds, it is well worth the effort. Don't trust the factory-set "automatic" settings. Automatic white balance is usually accurate for the first few months of use. However, over time, the setting's accuracy deteriorates. If you find yourself in a complex lighting situation (for example, fluorescent light overhead *and* sunlight coming in through open windows) make a test tape using the indoor, outdoor, and automatic settings. Watch the tape—remember, do *not* adjust the tint control on the TV set—and determine which white balance setting will produce the best picture.

Iris Controls. As we established earlier, the lens gathers and shapes the light from the physical environment. You may use a 12 x 1 lens to gather this light. This lens measures about 50 millimeters. However, the lens won't always be open its entire circumference. Within each lens is a lens iris, the mechanism which controls the lens opening, called the aperture (fig. 1.3). The aperture is measured in an industry-standard format—the f-stop. The f-stop is usually expressed as the letter *f* followed by a number. An example would be f/8. What this really means is f (aperture size) = one-eighth. In other words, the lens is open to one-eighth of its capacity. Most lenses on camcorders range from about f/1.5 to f/22. This allows for videography in nearly dark and very bright situations. In a darkened classroom, the aperture will probably be open as wide as the iris allows. But if you go outside on a sunny day, the aperture will become quite small (f/22)—about the size of the tip of a pencil. This change is usually performed automatically by the camcorder's automatic iris control. The automatic iris looks for the brightest part of the screen and automatically adjusts the aperture size to the appropriate level. By now you

Fig. 1.3. Lens aperture.

may have detected the potential flaw in the automatic iris control—the fact that the automatic iris keys on the brightest part of your video picture. What if the brightest part is *not* the subject of your shot? Unfortunately, the automatic iris cannot distinguish between what you mean to shoot, and what actually goes on the tape. Here's an example: You need to videotape a brief speech by the school principal, and because you want to convey a friendly tone, you have decided to videotape the principal sitting at her desk. The principal is seated in front of a plate glass window. The blinds are open and the beautiful sunny day provides an excellent background. Your camera's automatic iris control will adjust the aperture to the brightest spot in the picture—in this case, the sunny view through the window. Unfortunately, your principal will appear as a dark silhouette in front of the beautiful exterior view. Here's another example: Your school's art teacher has been asked to make a presentation at a state art convention. One of his new techniques involves working with color-tinted oils in a glass tray that is placed upon an overhead projector. To obtain the full effect, the art teacher uses the overhead projector as the only light in the room. You have decided to make a videotape of this technique to help your art teacher with his presentation. You probably know what will happen. The camcorder will record the overhead projector perfectly, but the teacher and students standing in the shot will appear as silhouettes. Even though such a shot will look bad through the viewfinder, even experienced videographers make the mistake of shooting the scene. Why? Because the room doesn't look that bad to the naked eye. The human eye can distinguish a contrast ratio of about 1,000 to 1; thus even if the brightest part of our view is 1,000 times brighter than the darkest part, we can still distinguish features of both parts. And if the ratio exceeds this level, our brains can search our personal experiences, allowing us to subconsciously "fill in the gaps." A photographic/motion picture camera can handle a contrast ratio of about 100 to 1. This is what gives motion pictures and professional photographs their beauty and depth. Unfortunately, video lags far behind at a 30 to 1 maximum ratio. That's why our two shots—the principal and the art teacher—looked so bad. We had exceeded the 30 to one contrast ratio, a ratio so small that we encounter contrast problems even when videotaping dark-complexioned people wearing light-colored clothing or standing in front of a white background. Video just can't handle it.

What do we do, then? Do we simply refuse to videotape in difficult situations? Of course not! There are three ways to solve the problem. One way is quite obvious—move the subject of your shot, or eliminate the problem area. In our first example, we could close the window shades or videotape the principal using a different part of her office as the background. This would allow the iris to adjust to the principal's face, rather than the sunny scene outside the window. But this doesn't work for our second example. That leads us to our second option—add more light. Our art teacher could probably perform his demonstration with the lights on. In our first example, a small video light could be pointed at the principal to bring the brightness of her face up to the brightness level of the view outside the window; a complete discussion of lighting beginning on page 38. The final solution involves the iris—either manually override the iris or calibrate it using a control on the camcorder. Most camcorders have one, if not both, of these features. The manual override enables the camera operator to turn the automatic iris off and adjust the iris manually, usually by twisting a knob. Calibrating the automatic iris keeps the automatic iris functional, but redefines the best level of light for the camera to process. This is usually operated with a dial on the camcorder marked "open" and "closed" on the extremes. Twisting the dial slightly to the "open" position makes all of the video brighter and maintains that setting when the camera is moved from indoors to outdoors; the auto iris still works, it just allows more light into the camera all of the time. Conversely, when the calibration is set to the "closed" position, the auto iris allows less light to enter the camera. Overriding or calibrating the automatic iris often causes more problems than it solves, however. Closing the iris usually gives the imaging device (tube or CCD) less light than it really needs to process a video signal. The result is a "snowy," colorless picture. Opening the iris past the automatic setting overloads the imaging device, distorting the picture and ultimately damaging the tube or CCD. An overloaded signal from a tube appears smeared. Video from an overloaded CCD appears orange/yellow, and often contains zebra stripes at its bright parts. There are, however, practical uses for manually controlling or calibrating the iris. The one that comes to mind involves a ballet dancer dancing in spotlight against a black background. Although the dancer's face and costume will probably be the brightest part of the shot, it may not be large enough (or stationary enough) to influence the iris setting. The result will be a grayish image of the black background and an overly bright dancer. Making the iris smaller, thus allowing less light in the camera, would normalize the brightness of the dancer and return the background to its natural black.

Let's return to our two examples: the principal's office window and the art teacher's projector demonstration. We could open the iris in the principal's office to brighten her face. But how would this effect the background? It would turn the office-window view into a sheet of solid white background. And what if the iris was opened in the classroom? The instructor and students conducting demonstrations would come into view, but the overhead projector view would be totally lost. So, the automatic iris function is usually used in videography. Poor composition situations are best solved by good camera skills, thoughtful planning, and the addition of simple lights.

Automatic Focus. Most camcorders on the market today have automatic focus (autofocus). Automatic focus makes fine-tuning adjustments in the lens focal length to allow your images to become sharp and clear without using a manual focus. The camera automatically focuses on the dominant part of the screen. This area is usually indicated in the camera viewfinder by a white rectangle. This focus area can be changed or even moved with some cameras. Automatic focus can be used most of the time during simple video shoots. But when the videographer wants to be more artistic or capture an unusual shot, automatic focus presents significant disadvantages. For example: You are videotaping bust shots of several outstanding students. Instead of centering each student in the shot, you decide to place them along the front third of the screen (see the section titled "Picture Composition," beginning on page 54) with the school serving as the background. Using automatic focus, your camera will focus on the school background, because your subject is not dominant in the center of the screen. In this case, you would need to use manual focus. Turn the automatic focus off and manually focus the camera using the focus ring on the lens. Here's another scenario: You are videotaping a second-grade class standing on stage singing a few songs during a school assembly. The students are standing in a single line, shoulder-to-shoulder, across the stage. You are near the middle of the assembly room with your trusty camcorder on a tripod. You maintain a complete shot of the class during the first song. For the second song, you decide to get a close-up of each singer. You slowly zoom to a close-up of the singer on the extreme left and your autofocus keeps the shot clean and clear. So far, so good. After a few seconds, you pan (side-to-side camera movement) the camera to the right to get a close-up of the next singer. Your camera is momentarily between the two singers and your autofocus adjusts to—the wall behind the singers! As you move to the second singer, the autofocus adjusts once again. The solution: Use the autofocus during the zoom, and turn it off once the first close-up has been achieved. As you move from singer to singer, your manual focus adjustments will be very slight, if they're needed at all. On the last singer, turn the autofocus back on and zoom out slowly to the full group shot. Here's a final autofocus scenario for you to solve: You are making an orientation tape for your school's new students and parents. You decide to begin the program with a shot of your school's beautiful exterior and large oak trees. As you videotape, a cool breeze blows, gently brushing a tree branch into the shot. What happens? Right! The autofocus adjusts to the branch, blurring the school in the background. In this case, establish the shot, and turn the autofocus off. Even a butterfly fluttering by can trick the autofocus. Videographers who are artistically inclined can probably think of good uses for the autofocus's lack of subjective judgment. The orientation tape described above could begin with the exterior shot of the school. The camera is placed on a tripod, the autofocus is turned off, and the focus on the camera is blurred. Then, roll tape, and after a few seconds, turn the autofocus on. Your school will come into focus, making a simple but eye-catching effect. Once again, thoughtful camera work and knowledge of your equipment will allow you to make the most of your camcorder's features.

Automatic Gain Control (AGC). As stated throughout this chapter, the imaging device (tube or CCD) converts the light that enters through the lens into an electrical signal. But what if there isn't much light with which to work? The result is a weak, noisy signal. Most video cameras offer a partial solution—the automatic gain control, or AGC. In video terms, *gain* means adjustment of level of signal. Automatic gain control on a camcorder will increase the level of the video signal when needed, automatically. AGC is usually needed in unexpected, low-light situations. (Had we known about the low-light situation, we would have brought a portable light, right?) At this point, the iris is all the way open, and we still don't have enough light. An example would be a school soccer match that is delayed or runs late. The sun sets, and the players can barely see the ball, but by using the automatic gain control on your camcorder, you can continue to videotape a reasonably good quality picture. Earlier, we stated that AGC amplifies a weak, noisy signal. Unfortunately, it then becomes a strong, noisy signal. The picture quality doesn't improve, it just becomes brighter. Experiment with the AGC in a dimly lit classroom. Watch the tape on a high-quality television set and determine which you like best—the darker, cleaner shot without AGC or the AGC shot that is brighter and noisier.

High-Speed Shutter. Most photography hobbyists understand how the still camera's shutter works. When the button is pushed to take a picture, the shutter opens for a fraction of a second to expose the film to light. If the action happens very quickly (someone riding a bicycle past the camera) the picture may be blurred, because the motion of the subject casts different light patterns on the film. On more advanced cameras, the shutter speed can be adjusted to provide a quicker shutter speed. In the example above, a shutter speed of 1/500 of a second should be sufficient to "freeze" the bicycle rider. Of course, the lens aperture must be enlarged to allow enough light into the camera. This same principle has been applied to video. Of course, a camcorder doesn't have a shutter; light is always allowed to enter the camera. (Even when the camera is off, light enters the camera through the uncapped lens and hits the imaging device.) Videographers who tape dynamic scenes (sports, wildlife action, etc.) like the high-speed shutter capability. So most camcorders are equipped with a high-speed shutter "effect." The control is often marked just like a still camera, with terms like 1/250, 1/500, and 1/1,000. In effect, the control actually divides the CCD into two or more parts, providing the camcorder with several signals per cycle, instead of just one. Confused? Don't worry about it. (After all, you don't have to know how to repair a watch to tell time, right?) The important thing here is to be aware of the advantages and disadvantages of the high-speed shutter feature. The advantage is the obvious picture quality improvement in fast-moving shooting projects. The pedaling feet of the bicycle rider will be sharp and clear, not blurry, if the high-speed shutter is used. The disadvantages are two-fold: (1) the high-speed shutter feature requires more light than normal camcorder operation and thus can only be used in bright situations; and (2) the high-speed shutter function can be accidentally activated by even experienced videographers—if the button is located on the "cheek side" of the camcorder, a big smile may turn it on and darken your shot! Just like all of the other features described, use high-speed shutter wisely in the proper situations.

Macro Lens. The macro lens is a separate lens located within the camcorder lens that allows videography of very small objects. Using the macro lens enables you to fill the screen with a small item such as a penny or a postage stamp. A standard lens won't be able to focus on any subject that is less than 2 or 3 feet from the camera; at that point, you will need to use the macro lens. This usually involves pressing a button on the lens and twisting a dial, but every camcorder is different so make sure to consult the owner's manual. Because the macro lens has a *very* short focal length, you can expect a great deal of the kind of barrel distortion that is produced by a wide-angle lens. A macro lens has an infinite number of uses in the elementary school setting. Teachers and students could make a videotape from postcards and photographs using the camcorder in the macro position on a tripod. Items that would ordinarily be too fragile to pass around among your students in class can be placed in front of the macro lens and shown on television. With a little thought, most teachers can think of many uses for a macro lens in the classroom.

Digital Zoom. As mentioned before, most camcorders have a zoom lens in the neighborhood of 12 x 1, which is more than adequate for most videotaping tasks. (In fact, very few videographers can hold a camera steady enough to use a 12 x 1 lens zoomed in all the way.) A digital zoom can increase the camera's zoom range without increasing the lens size or the focal length. As the name implies, the digital zoom takes the digital signal produced by the CCD, crops the outer portion on all sides, and enlarges the image to the standard picture size. A 20 x 1 digital zoom would be significantly closer than a 12 x 1 zoom. You can probably imagine the problem with such a powerful digital zoom: The resolution becomes mosaiclike. The digital zoom divides the screen into squares, eliminates the outermost squares, and enlarges the remaining squares. When the digital zoom requires those squares to be large, the resolution suffers. At this time, we cannot be sure if the digital zoom will become a standard feature on camcorders or just another passing video fad.

Fade Button. Another feature available on most camcorders is a fade button. This feature allows fading from a background color to the video shot, and from the video shot back to the background color. The color is usually black, but some camcorders offer a choice of other colors, including white. The fade button can be a nice touch at the end of an awards ceremony or school play videotape, but abuse of the fade button becomes tiresome and reminds the viewer of a dream sequence from a bad soap opera. Use with care and thought.

Tracking. The VCR portion of the camcorder has a few controls that need attention. One of those is tracking. The tracking control allows for adjustment of the placement of the videotape on the VCR heads. Tracking controls slightly misaligned will produce a videotape with a fuzzy bar along either the top or the bottom of the screen. Tracking totally out of line will produce an unwatchable picture. Many camcorders have a digital tracking control. Instead of being controlled with a dial, this tracking is controlled with buttons in a "+" or "-" configuration. An analog tracking control is a dial that can be adjusted to achieve optimum picture quality. When recording, the analog tracking control should be in the center position, usually indicated by a white notch on the dial. Both the analog and digital tracking controls are on the camcorder for use in the playback function. (Although we don't recommend it for long-term use, a camcorder can be connected to a television set and used as a VCR.) Some tapes recorded on other video systems require tracking adjustment in playback. Whether you have analog or digital tracking on your camcorder, the control should remain in the center position during recording, and adjusted only when a picture is distorted in playback.

Tape Speed. Most camcorders give the user the choice from among three standard speeds of recording. Those speeds are known as: Standard Play (SP), Long Play (LP) or Extended Play (EP), and Super Long Play (SLP). Most VHS videotapes purchased from a store will be marked T-120. This means that the tape will last 120 minutes (2 hours) on SP. The same tape would last 240 minutes (4 hours) on LP/EP, and 360 minutes (6 hours) on SLP. Recording at a slower speed may sound good economically, but the picture quality will suffer dramatically. Blank videotape is quite inexpensive; thus, unless an emergency arises, you should always use SP when recording with a camcorder. Slower speeds should be reserved for the situations when a program is lasting longer than expected and speed must be reduced in order to fit the entire event on your only tape. Most professional quality VHS machines will only play on the SP mode. If you have the opportunity to edit on professional equipment, any tapes recorded on the slower speeds will have to be converted to SP before editing.

Record Review. Record review allows the videographer to see the last few seconds of video recorded on the videotape without leaving the "record" function. Most camcorders have some sort of button to push or window to slide to activate the "record" function of the camcorder. If you want to check the last few seconds of video recorded on a tape that is recording, simply press the record review button. The camcorder will automatically switch to play/pause, search back about three seconds of videotape, and play for about two seconds before returning the camcorder to record/pause. This feature is great when you need to "make sure" that you actually recorded your last shot. However, careful readers probably detected a flaw in the preceding explanation. The tape is searched back about three seconds, but only rolls forward two seconds. What happens to the other second of tape? It is still there, but you'll record over it the next time you push the trigger. The reason for doing this is to avoid creating a "glitch," or a small section of unrecorded tape, on the video. A single glitch can ruin about 10 seconds of your video project. This one-second disparity doesn't pose a real problem unless (1) you press record review several times, erasing one second each time, or (2) you are a "trigger-happy" videographer—you stop recording immediately after your desired shot. Combining "trigger-happy" camera work with multiple checks using the record review button can erase just about all of the segment recorded! Remember, record review is a valuable tool but only when used properly and judiciously.

Other Camcorder Features

Camcorder features differ greatly from model to model. Before making your camcorder purchase, note some other features that may be available.

Automatic/Manual Choice. Under the promise of "easy to use," some camcorders are fully automated. As you have read above, sometimes it is necessary to switch to manual functions, such as iris control, white balance, focus, and tracking. Make sure that any camcorder you are considering purchasing allows selection of the manual settings, as well as fully automated functions. Many "fully automatic" camcorders are perfect for making home movies, but won't support serious videography.

Date/Time Recording and Character Generators. Most camcorders have a way of recording the day, date, and even time on the videotape. For the family historian, this might be a useful tool. But for use in schools, it can be more of a hindrance than a help. Having the date displayed on the screen as the video plays is charming at best, and quite annoying at worst. Other similar features include a stopwatch feature that puts the running time on the video. (Useful if your school participates in track meets, but otherwise of little use in the school setting.) Another feature is a built-in character generator that allows the programming of titles onto the screen. Many of these camera-based character generators are quite functional, allowing solid-colored and transparent backgrounds, letter sizing, and scrolling. This feature may be particularly useful to schools that do not have electronic character generation capabilities. But beware of inadvertently activating this feature. One student videographer worked hard to type "THE END" onto a graphics page of his camcorder, and anxiously awaited his opportunity to use it at the end of the school play. You can imagine the disappointment of the student when, at the conclusion of the play, he realized that he had recorded "THE END" superimposed over the entire performance.

Audio and Video Outputs. Some camcorders have jacks that allow for the audio and/or video signal to be taken from the camcorder and sent directly to a television set or a monitor (fig. 1.4). This feature could be useful in many ways. It allows the camcorder to be used as a VCR and facilitates immediate playback of recorded footage. Also, there are some instances in which making tape really isn't the objective. For example: Imagine that a science teacher is demonstrating an experiment, and for safety reasons, she needs all of the students to remain at their desks, instead of gathering around the demonstration area. The science teacher can put the camcorder on a tripod, adjust the zoom lens to get a nice close-up of the experiment, and run a cable from the output of the camcorder to a television set in the classroom. Using a signal splitter purchased from a local electronics dealer, she could even send the signal to other television sets around the classroom. Here's another use of the camcorder output:

Fig. 1.4. Camcorder outputs.

Imagine that a noted young adults' author is presenting a speech at your school. The audience will be 150 educators from around the district. A portable P.A. system guarantees that everyone will hear the author, but because your school doesn't have an auditorium or stage, you're concerned that not everyone will be able to see her. Your solution is to set up a camcorder about 15 feet from the speaker (you were probably going to record her speech anyway) and run a cable from the camcorder output to the input of a video projector. The video projector can be focused onto a screen to the side and behind the speaker, allowing everyone in the audience a clear view of her. The use of the output should in no way disturb the recording of the camcorder. At the end of the presentation, you will have a quality videotape, a satisfied audience, and the confidence that comes with the experience of learning more about your school's equipment.

Camcorder Formats. What might be considered a camcorder feature is the format of the videotape used by the camcorder. The dominant format in schools and in the retail market overall is the full-sized VHS format. The VHS format is the standard videocassette that most of us buy at the drugstore, rent at the video store, and record our favorite television shows on at home. Although the VHS format is the largest consumer camcorder tape currently used, it has one dominant quality: It is the status quo. This saturation basically guarantees that a tape that you make with your VHS camcorder can be viewed by just about anybody. Imagine that your district superintendent is so impressed by your school orientation tape that he wants to send a copy to the 10 other middle schools in your district so they can make their own tapes. (This is great, providing you cleared the copyright on the music!) If you make the copies on VHS, chances are the other schools will be able to view the tapes immediately. If you send a school a tape in another format—watch out! The school will probably have to obtain a VCR from another source just to watch your program. Realistically, in the busy world of education, your program probably won't get watched at all. The future may introduce a format that is better, smaller, and less expensive than VHS, but at the time of this writing, VHS is the standard accepted format.

Two other formats are somewhat compatible with VHS. They are S-VHS and VHS-C. An S-VHS videocassette looks identical in size and shape to a standard VHS videocassette. However, when an S-VHS cassette is used in an S-VHS camcorder and played back on an S-VHS VCR on a high-quality television, the results are dramatic. The picture is broadcast quality. You have probably already determined why the S-VHS format hasn't really caught on in schools or homes: In order to fully utilize the S-VHS format, *all* equipment must be S-VHS format. This may mean purchasing new camcorders, VCRs, and even televisions. To compound the expense, blank S-VHS tape costs about three times more than its VHS counterpart. S-VHS is not simply a high-quality VHS videocassette. It is a different tape that records signals in a different way. But even though conversion to this format would represent a substantial investment, S-VHS is not without its advantages. As stated before, S-VHS video is of broadcast quality. If you are preparing a videotape that will be broadcast by a television station, using S-VHS will certainly produce a better picture. (As you probably know, a copy of videotape doesn't look as good as the original, and a third generation tape [a copy of a copy] looks even worse.) VHS copies made from an S-VHS master tape look as good as a VHS original tape, because the S-VHS tape is so much stronger to begin with. Most high schools are now including both VHS and S-VHS formats in their television production studios, allowing for the creation of broadcast quality tape, as well as video projects that students can take home to share with their families. Once again, it is very important to clarify the compatibility issue. In order to record an S-VHS signal, you must use an S-VHS tape *and* an S-VHS camcorder. You *can* use an S-VHS tape to record with a VHS camcorder, but the result will be a standard VHS signal (see table 1.1). And an S-VHS tape cannot be played back on standard VHS equipment (see table 1.2).

Table 1.1. Videotape Recording Compatibility

Tape	+	Camcorder	=	Resulting Signal
VHS		VHS		VHS
VHS		S-VHS		VHS
S-VHS		VHS		VHS
S-VHS		S-VHS		S-VHS

Table 1.2. Videotape Playback Compatibility

Recorded signal	Playback VCR	Will it work?
VHS	VHS	Yes
VHS	S-VHS	Yes
S-VHS	VHS	No
S-VHS	S-VHS	Yes

Another format that is somewhat compatible with VHS is VHS-C. A VHS-C videocassette is about half the size of a standard VHS videocassette (see fig. 1.5). The VHS-C videocassette can be placed in a special adapter the size of a VHS videocassette and then inserted into a standard VHS VCR for playback. The smaller videocassette size allows the use of a smaller camcorder. The small camcorder may be tempting for elementary schools, especially if children will be using it. But the small format is not without problems. Although the small camcorder is lighter, it is more difficult to create a steady shot because of the absence of a shoulder rest. Holding the small, boxlike VHS-C camcorder up to the eye with only the hand as support becomes tiring and awkward, and playback of the VHS-C videocassette in a VHS VCR is only possible with the adapter. Lose the adapter, and the only option is to connect the camcorder directly to the television, using the camcorder as a VCR. Another problem arises if you plan to edit your VHS-C tape using professional VHS editing equipment. The videocassette adapter generally cannot withstand the physical strain put on tapes in the editing process. At least one manufacturer has created a VHS/VHS-C

Fig. 1.5. Videotapes—VHS, S-VHS (Back); Hi-8, VHS-C (Front).

VCR that eliminates the adapter, so there may be some relief in sight. However, at this point, the VHS-C format is better suited for family picnics and trips to Disneyland.

Other videocassette formats are making a dent in the video production business. The Hi-8 format offers a small videocassette and a high-quality picture. Although not at all compatible with VHS, Hi-8 is advancing in the marketplace because of aggressive marketing and the availability of Hi-8 VCRs and editing systems. The beta videocassette format continues to slip in popularity in the home market, but older machines are still available in some schools. A different beta format, Beta ED, is used by many television stations. Digital formats, such as D-I and D-II, are used by television and motion picture companies. Because this format encodes a digital, not analog, signal, a copy of it is of the same quality as the original. In fact, digital video copies are called "clones" in the video industry, because they are identical to the master tape. Thus far, digital videotape, which is not compatible with its standard cousins, hasn't made a dent in the elementary or middle school settings. But as video technology becomes less expensive, and therefore more accessible, we can expect exciting opportunities in the ability to educate using technology.

A Final Note on Camcorders

Remember to read your camcorder's instruction manual before you begin to use it at your school. Manuals are notorious for their brevity. But careful reading with the camcorder in hand and a professional contact just a phone call away can make learning about your camcorder almost as rewarding as using it to enhance the educational process.

Video Cameras/Video Decks

Up to this point we have focused almost exclusively on the camcorder. Schools usually purchase camcorders because of their relatively inexpensive price, automatic features, and ease of operation. However, many school districts create videotape systems consisting of separate video cameras and video decks; thus, the video camera and the video recording deck are independent items of equipment (fig. 1.6).

The video camera is about the same size and shape as the camcorder. The video deck is somewhat smaller than a home VCR. The video deck is technically not a VCR because it doesn't have a tuner. It cannot be programmed to receive or record standard television signals. The two components (camera and deck) are connected by a cable that really has 10-15 different cables inside. This cable, called a pin-connector, contains all of the audio and video connections that are needed to

Fig. 1.6. Student operating camera/deck system.

connect the camera to the deck. These signals include power, audio, and video. (The video camera usually gets its power from the video deck battery.) Once connected, the camera and deck function like a camcorder. The camera is usually held on the shoulder, or mounted on a tripod. The video deck can be held on the shoulder by a strap, or simply placed on the floor or on a table.

Separate Component Advantages

As camcorders have become more advanced, separate cameras and decks have lost the advantage of superior picture quality. There are four areas in which separate systems present somewhat of an advantage over camcorders: durability, ease of service, the ability to use each piece separately, and the availability of more professional features.

Because they are designed for use in a more professional/industrial setting, video cameras and video recording decks are often more durable than their camcorder counterparts. A metal alloy may replace the plastic used in camcorders, and screws will probably be used instead of glue. The professional system may include a hard case that would withstand a drop. Professional camera/deck systems are designed for everyday, heavy-duty use, as opposed to the average consumer camcorder, which is designed for occasional, light-duty use.

Professional camera/deck systems may also be easier to service. Because they are designed for use in a professional setting, they often allow easy access for in-house technicians. Professional systems are also more likely to include technical service manuals for use by school district or county repair personnel.

In the school setting, component cameras and decks can serve double duty. Because they aren't permanently joined to the video camera, video decks can be used to play tapes in classrooms, further familiarizing teachers with the video technology. Component video cameras can be connected directly to televisions for classroom use, or to consumer VCRs. Also, separate components are more convenient to repair. If the automatic focus malfunctions on a camcorder, the entire camcorder goes to the shop. With the component system, only the camera goes in for repair, while the video deck continues to provide service around the school.

Finally, the component system almost always has the automatic and manual features demanded by professional videographers. Automatic focus, auto iris, and white balance will all have manual overrides. The video deck will have easily accessible video and audio ins and outs, and will probably offer audio dub and video insert functions.

Separate Component Disadvantages

The most significant disadvantage in separate video camera and video deck components is cost. A medium-quality camera/deck system will cost three to four times as much as its camcorder counterpart. Most school media specialists would find it difficult to justify putting one system in a school when they could make four camcorders available to faculty and students.

Another consideration in the elementary/middle school setting is the size and weight of the camera/deck system. Very few students could be expected to comfortably carry both components. Placing a video deck on a table or on the floor seems to invite the possibility of damage, either through someone dropping or stepping on it.

Finally, if you have discovered some older (precamcorder) video equipment in your school, it is probably in the component camera/deck category. If the camera was made before the mid-1980s, it probably has a tube for an imaging device, which requires more light than the standard CCD camera. Because very few video tubes would last that long, you are probably looking at an expensive repair. Even if the repair is completed, the picture quality from such a camera would probably not meet your expectations. In short, camera/deck components currently in schools may be obsolete or in disrepair.

Industrial/Professional Videocassette Recorders

A certain group of videocassette recorders look similar to consumer models, but contain features not usually found on home VCRs. This category of VCR is often referred to as professional or industrial, denoting a midpoint in both price and power between the standard consumer VCRs found in homes and schools, and the broadcast equipment used in television production studios.

There are several distinct features of industrial/professional VCRs. One of the most visible features is a jog-shuttle wheel that allows pinpoint positioning of the videotape (fig. 1.7).

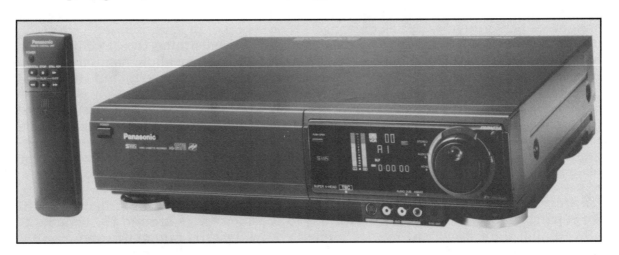

Fig. 1.7. VCR with jog-shuttle wheel. Photo courtesy of Panasonic.

The jog-shuttle wheel, a two-part "dial inside a dial," is usually located on the front of the VCR. There is usually a button located by the jog-shuttle wheel that activates the wheel, overriding the other VCR controls like play, fast-forward, and rewind. Once the button is pushed, the videotape inside the VCR goes into the play/pause position. In the center position, the dial gives a clean still/pause. When the outside dial is turned clockwise, the videotape searches forward. By gradually turning the dial clockwise, the forward search can be set for half speed, regular speed, double speed—up to a 10 times faster speed search or more, depending on the manufacturer and model. Once the desired tape position is found, the dial can be moved back to center to still/pause. Moving the dial counterclockwise activates a rewind search identical to the clockwise forward search. This is the "shuttle" function of the jog-shuttle wheel. The "jog" function is used by rotating the inside part of the wheel in a similar fashion. The jog function advances or rewinds a tape one frame at a time, which is useful for finding an exact location on a tape. To allow precise positioning, most jog dials have an indentation for placing a finger within the dial.

The clean still/pause described above is made possible by the presence of a fourth video head. As explained earlier in this chapter, the fourth "flying" head is activated when the VCR is placed on pause. All industrial/professional-level VCRs have four heads to allow for precise position of tapes and accurate editing.

Most industrial/professional VCRs can be connected to editing control units and/or have internal editing systems. Perhaps you have connected two VCRs together to edit or duplicate videotape that you have made around school. Industrial/professional VCRs allow this type of editing, and also accommodate a device known as an editing control unit, which is actually a microprocessor that can control the two VCRs, performing preprogrammed edits.

Industrial/professional VCRs usually have more audio and video inputs and outputs than standard consumer VCRs. Industrial/professional VCRs can accommodate a stereo signal and play a stereo videotape via stereo input and output jacks. With multiple video outputs you can connect the VCR to more than one monitor or VCR, a necessity in editing, as you need to send the video signal to both the recording VCR and a monitor.

Some of the better industrial/professional VCRs have built-in time-base correctors. A time-base corrector (TBC) is an electronic device that converts an inherently unstable signal from a video source (like a VCR) into a rock-solid video signal. This process is usually accomplished by digitizing the signal and instantly sending it down the line. Because it is shaping and redefining the signal anyway, most TBCs allow for manipulation of the signal, including signal strength, brightness, chroma (color) level, and color phase (hue). Therefore, in addition to stabilizing the signal, the industrial/professional VCR's TBC can help correct poor video quality. But don't confuse a time-base corrector with the "video enhancers" currently being marketed to consumers and video hobbyists. The TBC stabilizes the signal; picture adjustment is simply an added feature. Other "enhancers" connected between two editing VCRs may even reduce the quality of your finished video.

Finally, industrial/professional VCRs are generally more durable that standard consumer VCRs because they are designed for heavy-duty use in a business setting. To illustrate this point, let's say that a new high school receives a generous gift from a local discount department store: five consumer VCRs. The VCRs are checked out regularly by teachers and used almost continuously. After two years the five consumer VCRs will be worn out beyond financially feasible repair. At the same time, let's say the school purchases two industrial/professional VCRs for use in the school's television production department. With periodic cleaning, these VCRs can continue to provide excellent service after six years of constant student use. Ultimately, initial investment in quality equipment pays off even though the added features and durability of industrial/professional equipment do not come cheaply. Industrial/professional VCRs can cost up to five times more than their consumer counterparts. However, schools that engage in regular television production activities should consider purchasing at least one of these powerful tools.

Videotape

Just as important as the equipment used in video production is the videotape onto which you record your projects. The selection and use of videotape deserves careful attention.

Videotape Selection Criteria

Ancient wisdom tells us not to put new wine in old wineskins; similarly, we should not put our video projects on poor-quality videotape. Four important criteria can be used in evaluating the quality of blank videotape.

Company Reputation. This is probably the most important criterion for selecting blank videotape. In reality there are only a few companies in the world that actually manufacture blank videotape; other companies simply purchase the tape and market it under their own name. Most CEOs would probably agree that the company name is the most valuable asset of any corporation. Thus, in terms of video products, it is safe to say that the blank tape contained in that package will meet the quality standards of that company. Here's an example: For many years, one company has been on the forefront of film, paper, and processing for still photography. Not to be shut out of the video market, this company entered into an agreement to sell videotape with its name on the case. Needless to say, this is high-quality videotape; the company would settle for nothing less. It is interesting to note that most video equipment produced today is manufactured by Japanese corporations, where it is common for televisions, cars, and tennis shoes to all be marketed under the same name brand. Again, company name is the best criteria for videotape selection. If you have never heard of the company, chances are they aren't really serious about your videotape needs. Saving a dollar or two on a cheaper, off-brand tape may seem like a good idea, but you will ultimately pay in the areas listed below.

Picture Quality. Another criterion for tape selection is the picture quality that the videotape produces. If you're a beginner in videotape purchasing, you may have to ask a fellow professional or your local electronics dealer to recommend a tape. The picture quality will only be as good as the raw material that goes into the tape. Poorly made videotape may produce poor resolution and unacceptable color response.

Physical Durability. Another criterion for judging the worthiness of a blank videotape is the physical durability of the videocassette shell and the tape inside. In this case, you can learn a lot from "sacrificing" a tape to education. Open the trapdoor on top of the videocassette and pull out a section of tape. Stretch and pull as hard as you can. How far does the tape stretch before it breaks? Some tape will double, triple, even quadruple in length before it breaks. This is strong tape. Other tape will snap after a weak tug. This is not good tape. The first time your VCR drags a little bit, this poor-quality tape will break. Also, examine the tape that was stretched. Did the magnetic particles come off, leaving you with a handful of rust-colored dust? When tape is stretched its temperature rises. If the fixative and protective coating is of good quality, the particles will stay on the clear plastic base. Poor-quality fixative and coating will release the particles at the first sign of stress or heat. The result is metallic "dust" dropping off the tape and into your VCR. This will cause a drop-out—a momentary loss of picture—on your videotape. The dropped particles will probably make their way into your video head assembly, where they will damage and clog your VCR. Now as long as you've already trashed the videotape, drop it from waist level, then pick it up and shake it. Did it crack? Now stand on the plastic shell. Does it crack, splinter, or hold its ground? This may seem like an extreme experiment, but it speaks for the quality of the materials used in making this tape.

The company JVC holds the patent on the VHS videotape format and the copyright on the stylized VHS logo (fig. 1.8). Any company that sells VHS tape must pay a royalty to JVC for the use of the format and the logo. Displaying the logo also

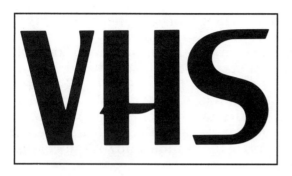

means that the tape adheres to industry standards for quality and durability. Note that not all blank videotapes display this logo; in addition, some companies pirate the logo, using it on their product, but not adhering to the standards. Reportedly, JVC and several other video companies have hired agencies and offered rewards for information about companies producing substandard videocassettes using the VHS logo. Once again, purchasing a major, well-known brand will usually guarantee a durable product.

Fig. 1.8. VHS logo.

Reuse Potential. This criterion may be a minor consideration to those who produce only a few programs that are shown only once or twice. But if your school produces programs that will be shown several times, be on the lookout for drop-outs. Make note of any tape brand that has caused distortion or partial erasure of your video projects.

Any tape used continuously will need to be replaced eventually. During a recent trip to a furniture store, one of the authors observed a videotape that played continuously. (The tape demonstrated the versatility of a sofa bed.) The three-minute program was full of snow, glitches, and drop-outs. Surely the store could request a new tape from the manufacturer. The biggest damage, of course, was to the VCR. A drop-out on the screen means that a substantial amount of metal particles has fallen off of the tape and into the VCR, potentially damaging the video heads and the tape mechanism. A good videotape should offer many excellent plays. But when the picture quality begins to suffer, obtain another copy of the program—either duplicate it if it was made at your school or purchase a new copy if it is a copyrighted program—and avoid expensive VCR repairs.

High-Grade Videocassettes. Most companies offer two or more "grades" of videotape. Disreputable companies use adjectives like "superior" and "high-grade" to describe their only tape. Honest, professional companies offer explanations of the differences between tape grades on the tape packaging. Generally speaking, higher-grade tapes work better than standard grades for camcorder and production use. The minimal extra cost is usually money well spent. Once again, critically view each tape that you make, noting the picture quality and the tape that produced it. As you gain experience in video production, you will develop favorite brands and grades of videotape.

Unfortunately, a few years ago a major consumer organization reported that no real differences exist in picture quality between grades of tape. Although this may be true for household videotape uses, it doesn't apply to video production. A higher grade usually results in a better picture.

Videotape Use

Even the best-quality videotape must be used properly. Here are some tips that will help you get the most out of your videotape investment.

Rewind and Fast-Forward First. Since the advent of the videocassette format, it has been a traditional precaution to fast-forward and rewind each videocassette before its initial use. The thinking behind this is that any physical tape problem or defect will reveal itself before a program has been recorded. The process takes only a few minutes, and if even just one defective tape is found in your lifetime, the time has been well spent. An initial fast-forward and rewind also "loosens up" a videotape that may have been stored for months, even years, in warehouses and stockrooms. One addition to this tradition would be to use a stand-alone fast-forward/rewind machine for this process to avoid unnecessary wear and tear on your VCR. When selecting a separate tape rewinder, make sure that it has a "slow-down" mechanism that reduces the rewind/fast-forward speed as the tape reaches the end. (Most VCRs perform this function.) Rewinding all the way back to the beginning of the tape at full speed could snap the end of the tape off of the spindle and/or put enough tension on the tape to cause particle drop-off.

Beware of the Sticker-Filled Tape. Most blank videocassette packages contain a plethora of stickers and labels for use by the consumer. The face and spine labels can usually be applied without problems. However, those are the only stickers that need to go on the tape! Certain manufacturers include small numeral stickers, and even small stickers with drawings representing any number of subjects that you may choose to record on your tape. These stickers can be used on the slipcase, but should not be attached to the videocassette itself. The heat of the running videotape can melt the glue, loosen the sticker, and cause the entire gooey mess to smear inside your VCR. You wouldn't put gasoline stickers in your gas tank during a fill-up, would you? Don't put videotape stickers inside your VCR!

Store the Master; Circulate a Duplicate. Once you have produced a videotape for school use, don't make the mistake of circulating the master tape that you have recorded. Instead, make a duplicate tape by connecting two VCRs together. Store the master tape and circulate the duplicate. Then, if the tape is lost, stolen, or simply wears out from use, you can make another copy from the master.

Environmental Hazards. Use the slipcase provided with the videocassette for storage. Dust that accumulates on a videocassette can damage the VCR.

Store the videocassette at room temperature. Avoid extremes in temperature, especially heat.

Do not store videocassettes near a magnetic source, like a television or a VCR. Erasure is improbable, but possible.

Do not open the plastic shell or touch the tape itself. Oil from the skin can damage the tape and the VCR heads. And anyone who has ever taken a videocassette apart knows that they are nearly impossible to get back together!

A quality videocassette can go a long way in creating an enjoyable television production project. Careful selection and thoughtful use of videotape can yield excellent results.

Monitors and Televisions

To watch your video programs you can use either a monitor or a television. You might think that a monitor is just a professional name for a television set, but this is not true. There are some significant differences between a television and a monitor.

Television and Monitor Differences

Televisions and monitors are obviously more similar than they are different. They both perform similar functions in the television production process. In fact, televisions in schools are frequently used as monitors. There are, however, two differences between televisions and monitors: the presence of a tuner and the type of signal processed.

The Role of the Tuner. A television set really consists of two parts: the cathode ray tube, better known as the picture tube, and the tuner. The tuner on a television receives television RF (radio frequency) signals that are broadcast through the air. It may get some assistance in receiving those signals from an antenna, a cable TV system, or a satellite dish. The tuner distinguishes the desired signals by consulting the channel that the viewer has selected. The tuner then splits the signal into audio and video, sending the audio signal to a small amplifier and then to the small speaker on the television, and sending the video signal to the cathode ray tube (CRT) to produce the picture. In summary, the tuner receives the signal, filters undesirable signals, and sends the audio and video signals to the audio speaker and picture tube.

Television sets have tuners; monitors don't. A video monitor is simply a CRT (picture tube) in a housing with controls like brightness, color, and contrast to adjust the response of the picture tube. Can you connect an antenna to a monitor and watch a broadcast program? No. The monitor has no tuner, and is not equipped to receive broadcast signals. Can you connect a cable TV feed to a monitor and watch cable programming? No, because there is no tuner. A monitor is equipped to receive a video signal, not an RF (radio frequency), which brings us to the second difference between monitors and televisions.

Radio Frequency Signal and Video Signal. As the above explanation indicates, televisions can receive RF (radio frequency) signals, while monitors can receive only video signals. There are some major differences between the two types of signal.

1. Power. The RF signal is much more powerful than the video signal. An RF signal can travel through a cable for miles. A video signal starts to lose strength after 30 or 40 feet.

2. Cable requirements. The RF signal is so powerful that it requires heavy-duty, insulated cable, commonly referred to as coaxial cable. The video signal can travel through ordinary shielded cable, like the cable used to connect stereo components.

3. Content. The RF signal contains both the audio and video portions of the program. The video signal contains only the video portion.

4. Point of origin. The RF signal is produced by transmitters at television stations; it can also be modulated by VCRs and satellite dish systems. The video signal is produced by video cameras and other video sources, like character generators, video switchers, video disc players, computers, and video games.

Converting Signals

You many encounter a situation that requires signal conversion, from RF to video signal or from video signal to RF. In other words, you need a monitor and all you have is a television, or vice versa. Let's return to an example used earlier in this chapter. A science teacher is conducting an experiment for a class, and because of the concern for safety, all students remain in their seats. Earlier, we put a camcorder on a tripod, focused on the experiment area, and connected the camcorder output to the television set. Now you know that the camcorder (actually, the video camera in the camcorder) produces a video signal, but the television set requires RF. To solve this problem, an RF modulator can be connected between the camcorder video output and the television set. The RF modulator converts the weak video signal into the RF signal needed by the television's tuner. Some RF modulators are even reversible, meaning that they can also convert the RF to a video signal. RF modulators are often included in the camcorder accessory package. Electronics stores sell RF modulators as well.

Differences in Quality and Price

Monitors usually rate higher in both quality and price than television sets. Because they process video signals, monitors are used almost exclusively by video production studios. With the absence of a tuner, shouldn't the monitor be cheaper? That makes sense, but the increased picture quality demanded by the video production situation makes monitors more expensive.

Fortunately, many televisions on the market today are actually combination television/monitors. The television has both RF and audio/video signal inputs. By flipping a switch, you can select either RF or audio/video input. These television/monitor combinations are quite popular in classrooms, especially in schools that are active in video technology. Because the combination sets produce only a standard television quality picture, the price is only slightly more than the average television set.

Microphones

Most, if not all, camcorders and video cameras have a microphone installed near the front of the camera body. This microphone is great for recording ambient sounds—the sounds that occur or are being produced in the recording environment, like the sounds of birds singing in the forest or the din of a school cafeteria. But even the video novice knows that this installed microphone is not suitable for recording more specific, important sounds, like a piano recital, a guest speaker's presentation, or the dialog of a school play. All too often, the camcorder is placed unobtrusively in the back of the room, with the expectation that the camcorder microphone will perform all of the audio tasks. Many school videographers have learned this lesson the hard way, recording an adequate picture, but tinny, echoing audio. The solution to this problem is to use an external microphone in place of the camcorder's installed microphone.

Just as most camcorders and video cameras have installed microphones, most also have installed a jack for an external microphone. Once again, in almost all cases, the jack is located near the microphone itself, and insertion of a microphone plug into the jack disables the mounted camcorder microphone. (See a discussion of the jacks and plugs used in videography on pages 33-34 and 41.) Earlier in this chapter, we defined a video camera as a device that converts light into electrical energy. A microphone is a device that converts sound waves into electrical energy. Just as light enters the camera through the lens, sound waves enter the microphone through the opening in the top of the microphone. Even though they are invisible, sound waves are quite active. Using the example of a pebble dropped into a bowl of water, we can make the same conclusions about sound waves. Anything that disturbs the surface, whether the surface be water or air, creates waves. Sound waves in the air are collected by the microphone and converted into electricity. The electricity travels down a cable and is recorded simultaneously with the video signal onto the videotape.

Microphones used in videography require careful selection. Although they are quite similar in appearance they can perform very differently in the field. You should consider three microphone characteristics when selecting a microphone for purchase or use. They are (1) microphone element, (2) microphone pickup pattern, and (3) microphone use conditions.

Microphone Element

Earlier, we stated that a microphone converts sound into electrical energy. The microphone element is the part of the microphone that actually performs this task. There are two types of microphone elements used in most microphones today: the dynamic element and the condenser element. They differ in their composition, performance, and power requirements. The dynamic microphone is used most often by news reporters and videographers who are recording speakers and presentations. In other words, the dynamic microphone is appropriate for recording the spoken word. Dynamic microphones can also withstand a moderate amount of physical shock. This abuse might include someone shouting into the microphone, placing the microphone near a booming bass drum, or accidentally dropping it. Dynamic microphones are usually priced affordably, starting at less than $50. The downside of the dynamic microphone is its inability to capture the full audio spectrum. The dynamic microphone does a fine job with mid-range tones, like those used in the spoken word, but is incapable of transferring very high and very low notes. A dynamic microphone wouldn't do a very good job of recording a duet between a piccolo and a tuba. But it represents a wise and economical choice for the videographer who desires a durable microphone for recording the spoken word.

The condenser microphone element also converts sound waves into electrical energy. However, a condenser microphone is capable of transferring most of the sounds audible to the human ear. Condenser microphones are used in recording studios, concert halls, and radio station booths. A videographer who records music or wants to capture a full, rich sound should use a condenser microphone when possible. Condenser microphones are naturally more expensive than dynamic microphones, starting at about $75. Because they are more sensitive than their dynamic counterparts, they are also more fragile. Condenser microphones should be used carefully to avoid damage. Another difference between dynamic and condenser microphones is in their power supply. Dynamic microphones receive the little power they need from the video camera or camcorder; condenser microphones require a power supply. That power supply is usually a battery that is installed in the microphone handle or in a box located on the microphone cable. The batteries range from 9-volt to hearing-aid size. Some condenser microphones designed for use in recording studios get their power directly from audio-mixing consoles. However, most microphones used in schools will require a battery. These battery-powered condenser microphones are called "electret condenser" microphones. The battery requirement really isn't a disadvantage, but it does require an extra measure of preparation. Most electret condenser microphones require a battery that has most of its power. Battery life is often quite short, and the microphone will not work *at all* without a battery. A videographer who videotapes piano recitals and chorus concerts should invest in a condenser microphone.

As a review, the dynamic microphone is economical, durable, and good for recording the spoken word. The condenser microphone is more expensive, more fragile, requires a battery, and is capable of providing full, rich sound over most of the audio spectrum.

Almost all microphones found in schools will fit into one of these two element categories. However, there are some microphones that you may have that are different. *Very* inexpensive microphones may have ceramic, or even wax paper-type, elements. As you can imagine, the sound produced is neither professional nor flattering. On the other end of the scale, very expensive microphones found in recording studios may have a ribbon element. In recent years, technological development has gone into making the condenser microphone the equivalent of the ribbon microphone.

Remember, *selection* is the key here. In a school setting, it is preferable to have both a dynamic *and* a condenser microphone available for your use.

Microphone Pickup Patterns

Just as microphones can be constructed from elements that perform very differently, they can also be designed to pick up specific parts of the physical environment. It's not enough just to make sure that the microphone is close enough to the source. Just as important is the type of pickup pattern, or area of reception, that your microphone has.

In a general sense, there are only two types of microphone pickup patterns: omnidirectional and unidirectional (fig. 1.9). As its name implies, the omnidirectional pickup pattern picks up sound from all around the microphone. A good omnidirectional microphone has a pickup pattern of about 360 degrees. This type of microphone can be good in a number of situations. For example, a quartet singing onstage could share a single omnidirectional microphone. A student interviewing a teacher could collect all of the sound for the interview without moving the microphone back and forth. Omnidirectional microphones are also good for collecting natural sounds, like the sound of a forest or a baseball game.

The unidirectional pickup pattern describes microphones that have been built to process much more sound from the front than from the sides. A unidirectional microphone can be thought of as a "sound flashlight" because it has to be pointed at the source of the sound. Because of the shape of its pickup pattern, a unidirectional microphone is also called a cardioid microphone. The illustration shows a basic cardioid pickup pattern, but the pattern can also be more narrow. Some microphones are described as super-cardioid, hyper-cardioid, or ultra-cardioid because they process sound almost exclusively from the front of the microphone. Unidirectional/cardioid microphones should be used when only a single source is desired on the recording. An example might be a poet reading several selections, or the song of a single bird in nature. News reporters often use unidirectional microphones to exclude loud background noise. A reporter recording a video news story at a football game or a construction site would definitely need a unidirectional/cardioid microphone.

Once again, you should be able to *select* the appropriate microphone pickup pattern for the given situation. It would be wise for a school to own both an omnidirectional and a unidirectional microphone.

At this time, it is important to point out that each microphone can be distinguished by its element *and* its pickup pattern. In other words, there are basically four types of microphones:

- dynamic omnidirectional

- dynamic unidirectional

- condenser omnidirectional

- condenser unidirectional

Here is a typical use for each microphone:

- dynamic omnidirectional: interviewing a group

- dynamic unidirectional: a speech by a single person

- condenser omnidirectional: a quartet singing onstage

- condenser unidirectional: a saxophone solo

You can probably think up many more uses for these microphones.

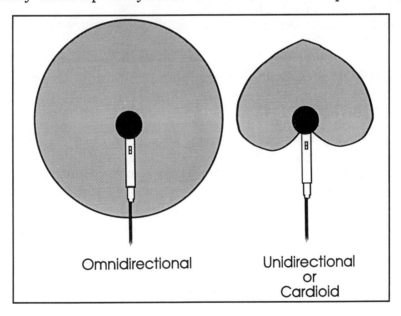

Fig. 1.9. Microphone pickup patterns.

Most microphones installed on camcorders and video cameras are condenser omnidirectional. Now you know that this is a good microphone for collecting ambient sound, but it doesn't really help when you're trying to record a speech or a school play.

Microphone Use Conditions

Aside from specially designed microphones, which we'll discuss later, there are two types of microphone design: the hand-held and the lavaliere. As its name indicates, the hand-held microphone is designed to be held by the performer. The performer may be a reporter, a guest speaker, a singer, or a narrator. The correct placement for a hand-held microphone is 6 inches from the source. Hand-held microphones can also be placed on floor stands or desk stands. A gooseneck allows easy positioning of a stand-based, hand-held microphone.

A lavaliere microphone is very small (see fig. 1.10). Lavaliere microphones are often called "tiepin" microphones because of their size. Lavaliere microphones can be used in many situations where hands-free operation is desired. A lavaliere microphone can also be gently taped to an acoustic (unamplified) musical instrument to provide clear recording. Because of their small size, most lavaliere microphones are of the condenser type. The battery is usually found in a small box connected to the microphone cable. Cor-

Fig. 1.10. Lavaliere microphone.

rect lavaliere microphone placement is about 6 inches from the source of the sound. A lavaliere microphone is a valuable addition to a school's audiovisual collection.

Special-Design Microphones

Four types of microphones are seen less frequently than hand-held and lavaliere microphones. They are designed for use in special circumstances. They are shotgun microphones, wireless microphones, surface mount microphones, and pressure zone microphones (PZM).

Shotgun Microphones. Earlier we talked about super-, hyper-, and ultra-cardioid microphones. These highly directional microphones are called shotgun microphones. The name, of course, implies the need to aim the microphone at a very specific subject and also relates to the microphone's long, slender appearance (fig. 1.11).

If three people are standing shoulder to shoulder 25 feet from the microphone, the microphone operator should be able to pick up each person singularly, with very little background noise from the other two. Obviously, this microphone requires careful use. Missing your aim by a few degrees can cause your audio to become faint and garbled. Headphones are required for proper shotgun microphone use.

Wireless Microphones. Wireless microphones can be used when stringing a length of microphone cable is impossible, impractical, or just plain dangerous (see

Fig. 1.11. Shotgun microphone.

fig. 1.12). For example, imagine you are videotaping a performance by your school's glee club. Your camcorder is stationed in the middle of the room, allowing you to get a good shot of the stage, but you want to position your microphone closer to the stage to get better sound. Naturally, you're worried about the entire school walking past the microphone cable you have laid along the floor. The solution is to use a wireless microphone. A wireless microphone uses radio waves to transmit a signal from a small transmitter, usually located within the microphone handle, to a receiving station located near the camcorder. The receiving station is tuned to the frequency of the microphone's transmission. A cable can connect the receiving station to the microphone input of the camcorder.

A wireless microphone can make an excellent addition to an elementary or middle school's media center. However, because of the wide range available for purchase and the precise nature of wireless microphones, it is important to point out three criteria for selecting a wireless microphone system. The first criterion is the range of the microphone; in other words, how far will the signal transmit. Try to anticipate all of the situations that will require the use of your wireless system, and estimate the distance that you would need the signal to transmit. Many inexpensive systems have ranges of less than 30 feet, which would certainly rule out their use in many situations. More professional systems boast ranges of a quarter mile or more. It is important to realize that manufacturers' estimates of wireless microphone range are made under optimum conditions, and may not reflect the system's performance in your situation. To obtain the maximum range you must have a direct "line of sight" between the transmitter and the receiving station. Walls, trees, and even the electricity from

Fig. 1.12. Wireless microphone system.

fluorescent lighting systems can cause the range of a wireless microphone to shrink dramatically. A second consideration for wireless microphone purchase is the frequency used by the system. Frequencies used for wireless microphones usually fall within the range of 49 mHz (megahertz) to 200 mHz. The higher the frequency, the better the quality of the sound. Many inexpensive systems use a 49 mHz frequency resulting in a poor-quality "walkie-talkie" sound. A frequency above 170 mHz is generally considered appropriate for professional settings. A final wireless microphone criterion is the quality of the actual microphone. The microphone—its design, sound quality, and pickup pattern—should meet the criteria that you apply to all of your microphone purchases. In sum, a good wireless microphone system should use a high-quality microphone, operate on a high frequency, and meet the range needs of your program.

Surface Mount Microphone. Many businesses, churches, and schools have installed surface mount microphones in auditoriums and conference rooms (see fig. 1.13). As the name implies, surface mount microphones are designed to be mounted on a flat surface, such as a ceiling, a wall, or a table. Surface mount microphones have a flat back and can be mounted with double-sided tape or screwed into place. Surface mount microphones may prove useful if you tape many programs in your school's auditorium, or tape conferences while the participants are seated around a table.

Fig. 1.13. Surface mount microphones. Photo courtesy of Shure Brothers, Inc.

Pressure Zone Microphone (PZM). A PZM takes the surface mount idea one step further, making the surface part of the microphone (see fig. 1.14). A PZM is a small microphone facing toward a metal plate. The plate picks up the vibrating airwaves, creating a "pressure zone," and transfers the vibrations to the microphone. Any surface that comes in contact with the plate becomes part of the pressure zone. Therefore, if the PZM is placed on a table, the table becomes part of the pressure zone, and any sound waves that hit the table are transferred to the microphone. Obviously, the waves diminish somewhat over distance, so a source closer to the

Fig. 1.14. Pressure zone microphone.

microphone is stronger than one farther away. Because the PZM plate is made of highly conductive metal, the sound of the microphone can be somewhat metallic. Also, when using the PZM, the talent must be aware of the negative effects of tapping a pencil on the desk or table. Still, the PZM can work well while recording students or adults sitting at a conference table, or working at a coffee table or activity center.

Microphone Impedance and Microphone Adapters

School videographers are often faced with an annoying situation: The connector at the end of the microphone doesn't fit the microphone jack on the camcorder. There may be one of two problems: The first problem, that of impedance, must be corrected electronically; the second problem is one of simply adapting the microphone to fit the jack.

Microphone Impedance. Impedance is the amount of resistance an electronic signal generates as it travels down a cable length. In other words, how hard does the signal fight? In a very general sense, microphones can be classified as either high-impedance (Hi-Z) or low-impedance (Low-Z). Without going into the history or reasoning, most professional/broadcast quality microphone systems are low-impedance (Low-Z). Low-Z microphone equipment generally gives better sound quality, and the microphone cable can be very long with very little signal loss. Most microphones used in industrial/consumer/school-based video production are high-impedance (Hi-Z). Almost all camcorders use Hi-Z audio. Hi-Z microphone equipment is generally less expensive than its Low-Z counterparts and still offers good sound quality. As you have probably guessed, Hi-Z and Low-Z microphones and mixers are not compatible with each other.

Most, but not all, Low-Z microphones have three-pronged XLR connectors (fig. 1.15). A videographer will quickly find that the camcorder has no jack that looks anything like the XLR plug. If, after reading the microphone manual, you determine that the microphone indeed is Low-Z, you must use an impedance adapter. Impedance adapters are barrel-shaped, cigar-sized devices that convert low-impedance signal to high-impedance signal, and vice versa. Connecting an impedance adapter to our Low-Z microphone will change the impedance, allowing it to be used with our camcorder. Remember, the problem is not simply the size and shape of the connector. The problem is in nonmatching impedance. An impedance adapter sells for less than $20. A simple adapter (discussed below) that changes the XLR to fit the camcorder costs less than $5. The temptation is to buy the less expensive adapter, but it won't solve the impedance problem.

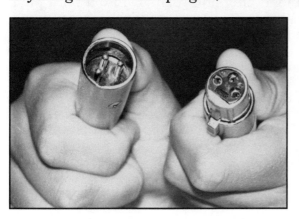

Fig. 1.15. XLR connectors.

Now you may be asking the question, "Why would I buy a microphone that doesn't fit the impedance of my camcorder?" Those of us who have worked in schools know that equipment is as much a function of legacy as it is selection. You may be able to obtain surplus microphones from the district media center or other schools in the district, or business or community members may donate Low-Z microphones. The purchase of a $15 impedance adapter may garner a slightly used, professional quality microphone for your school's video production collection.

Microphone Adapters. In most cases, incompatible impedance will not be your problem. Both the camcorder and the microphone will be Hi-Z, but the plug at the end of the microphone will simply not fit the microphone jack on the camcorder. The solution is to purchase a microphone adapter. The two dominant connectors in microphones are "phone" and "mini" (figs. 1.16 and 1.17). The phone jack, also

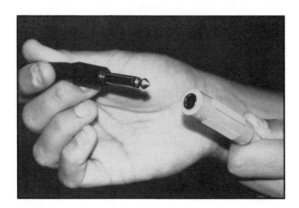

Fig. 1.16. Phone connector.

Fig. 1.17. Mini connector.

known as ¼-inch (diameter), is the standard connector used in stereo system headphones. The mini connector, also known as a ⅛-inch mini connector, is commonly used in portable stereo equipment. Unfortunately for the camcorder user, most microphones use phone connectors, and most camcorders use mini jacks. A simple adapter that accepts the phone plug and turns it into a mini plug can be purchased at electronics shops for less than $5. Be aware of the stereo/mono distinction. If you are using a standard microphone with a standard camcorder, you will need a mono (single-channel) adapter designed specifically for microphone use. (Most microphones and camcorders are mono/single-channel. Occasionally, you may encounter a stereo camcorder or stereo microphone. If you are unsure, consult your owner's manual.) The alternative is the stereo adapter, which would be used to adapt a pair of headphones with a phone plug for use in a personal stereo with a mini jack. Using the stereo adapter with your mono microphone and mono camcorder could result in signal loss. The best bet is to ask questions and read labels and manuals.

Microphone Wish List

At this point, we would like to offer of list a microphones that we think would be useful to your school. The microphones are listed in order of anticipated use and value to your program.

1. hand-held, dynamic, unidirectional microphone

2. lavaliere, condenser, omnidirectional microphone

3. hand-held, dynamic, omnidirectional microphone

4. hand-held, condenser, unidirectional microphone

5. shotgun, condenser, super-cardioid microphone

6. pressure zone microphone (PZM)

7. wireless microphone system; either lavaliere or hand-held, depending on anticipated need.

This list should be adapted to your specific situation. However, purchasing the microphones above as money becomes available (i.e., possibly one or two new microphones each year) will build a complete, useful microphone collection.

Tips for Microphone Use and Care

Using microphones successfully is a result of experience and education. Here are some tips to avoid disappointing experiences and broken, abused microphones.

Mic a Source, Not an Area. This is a standard rule for using microphones. Whenever possible, use a microphone to record a specific source, not just an area in which the sound occurs. For example, if you are recording a guest speaker who has come to your school to talk to your sixth-graders about fire safety, you could set the camcorder at a comfortable distance and use the installed camcorder microphone. However, this would be mic.ing the area, not the source. What you would get would be an echoing sound of the guest speaker, shuffling feet, and the sound of the occasional late student entering the room. In order to get the best sound quality, you would need to mic the source. In this case, a directional microphone placed on the lectern would suffice. Or if the speaker walks while speaking, an unobtrusive lavaliere microphone could be used.

Beware of Microphone Handling Noise. Hands rubbing against a microphone make a terrible rumbling sound. Educate your speakers, and use lavalieres and shotgun microphones when possible.

Handle Your Microphones Carefully. The applied rule is to handle a microphone like an egg. You can carry an egg, put an egg in your pocket, and even store an egg in a padded case. However, you shouldn't drop an egg, throw an egg, or pound the top of an egg. Never test a microphone by blowing, spitting, or pounding it. Instead, speak normally into the microphone. Handle your microphones with care. Microphone abuse may mean spending this year's A/V budget on a new hand-held microphone, instead of that new shotgun microphone you've been eyeing!

Beware of Microphone Cable Abuse. Breaks in the microphone cable can render a microphone useless. Carefully coil microphone cable when not in use. There is no need to tightly wrap the cable, or twist it around the microphone body. Do not hang your microphones by the cable for storage purposes. Most repair shops will charge at least $25 to open a microphone for repair, let alone make an expensive cable repair. So keep the cable loose.

Always Use Headphones. When using an external microphone, *always* use a pair of headphones to monitor the audio. Most camcorders offer a headphone jack. Use it. Many microphones have on/off switches. If the videographer is not monitoring the audio, the entire audio portion may go unrecorded.

Microphone use should be a process of careful selection and professional execution. Everyone involved in video production at your school should know the element type, pickup pattern, and impedance of each microphone in your collection. The correct use of microphones can go a long way in making your school-based video productions more professional and watchable.

Fig. 1.18. Video camera on a tripod.

Mounting Equipment

When an absolutely steady shot is required in video production, or when the video assignment is so long that the videographer will become tired holding a camera in one position, a mounting device can be used. Mounting devices steady the camera and also provide tireless service.

Tripods

A tripod is a three-legged, portable, collapsible mounting device (fig. 1.18). Tripods are used frequently in video production, and should be considered as important to the video production process in certain situations as a camcorder and a good microphone. The tripod is invaluable when shooting extended interviews, school or class programs, and guest speakers. Even the strongest, best videographer will find it impossible to hold a steady shot for more than a minute or two.

A tripod allows two basic mounting device camera movements: the pan and the tilt. The pan is a side-to-side motion of the camera on top of the tripod. A pan can be used to include or exclude certain subjects from your shot, or follow the action of a moving subject. A tilt is an up-and-down camera movement. A complete tilt of a person, beginning with the feet and moving to the top of the head, can have humorous results. Make sure that tilting is not abused, especially when videotaping short children. It is easy to set the camera on a tripod and tilt down to get a shot of the child. However, the downward slant of the shot emphasizes the top of the head and makes the subject seem more diminutive than he or she really is. Instead, shorten the tripod legs and place the camera at the student's eye level.

When purchasing a tripod, make sure that the tripod is designed for video cameras. Many tripods that are acceptable for lighter still-photography cameras cannot withstand the weight of the video camera. Most tripods display a maximum weight allowance in the instructions. Before shopping, weigh your camera (or consult the owner's manual) and make this your prime evaluative criterion. Saving a few dollars on a tripod may produce disastrous results when the tripod collapses under the weight of your camera. Three other selection criteria should be the height range of the tripod, the collapsed size, and the number of loose pieces. Make sure that your tripod has the height range that you need. Will it adjust low enough to videotape your shortest students and tall enough for the tallest adult? If you are doing video work outside the school building, you should consider the collapsed tripod size. Will the tripod fold up small enough to easily transport to a remote location? Or will the tripod become a burden that the videographer will leave at the school? Finally loose pieces (screws, bolts, etc.) are easily lost, especially in the school setting. Select a tripod that will not jettison essential parts.

The Tripod Dolly

A dolly can be added to most tripods to provide the feature of rolling as well as extra stability for your tripod base (fig. 1.19). Tripod dollies designed for use with camcorders usually consist of three metal "arms" with caster on each end. The tripod is attached to the dolly with a screw-post system or a more common rubber tie-in. Each tripod leg is placed directly over a caster to increase the stability of the camcorder.

The addition of a tripod dolly facilitates two more camera movements: the truck and the dolly. A truck is a side-to-side motion of the tripod dolly, similar to the tripod pan but with a different result. While the pan gives the effect of a head turn, the dolly gives the impression of an entire body movement. Imagine that you are videotaping the second-grade class singing a holiday song. All of the students are lined up across the front of the stage. To get a close-up of each student, you could pan, but the result would be uneven close-ups because of the unequal distances between each student and the camera. Trucking, using a tripod dolly, in a straight line parallel to the stage would add a dynamic "moving camera" effect. Another tripod dolly camera movement is the dolly. A dolly is a forward-and-back-

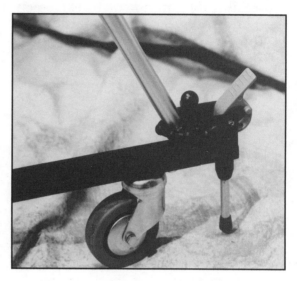

Fig. 1.19. Tripod/dolly connection.

ward movement of the tripod dolly. The terms *dolly-in* and *dolly-out* are used to describe moving the tripod dolly toward the subject and away from the subject, respectively. Unlike the camera zoom, which expands the centermost part of the screen to fill the screen, the dolly-in actually takes the viewer closer to the location. Once again, the moving-camera aspect is quite dramatic.

A good dolly costs about as much as the tripod itself. When shopping for a dolly, consider the firmness of the tripod/dolly connection, the ease with which the casters roll along the floor, and the ability to disable the casters by "locking down" the dolly. Although a dolly may seem an unnecessary frill to a television production program, it will pay for itself the first time a tall parent sits in front of your camcorder at the school play and you can simply r-o-l-l out of the way!

The Monopod

As the name indicates, a monopod is a single-legged mounting device (fig. 1.20). Of course, the monopod will not support the camera; this would defy the laws of gravity! Instead, the monopod is designed to support the weight of the camcorder, while allowing maximum portability and videographer control. Monopod legs are adjustable, so they can be used by a videographer who is seated or standing.

Mounting equipment is extremely important in establishing a professional look for the video production. Every school should own a tripod for each camcorder, and consider the purchase of at least one dolly and one monopod.

Fig. 1.20. Monopod.

Lighting

Because a video camera converts light into electrical energy, it is important to supply the camera with enough light to do the job. Also important is the placement of that light and the type of light that the camera processes. You may be thinking that your student news shows are quite simple and don't require elaborate lighting designs. You're probably right, but knowledge of the concepts of lighting will help your entire video production. After reading this section, you may decide to add one or two lights to really enhance the look of your recordings.

White-Balancing the Camera

As you read earlier in this chapter, white balance is very important to the operation of the camera. Even if your camcorder offers only a choice of "indoor" and "outdoor," it is still worthwhile to carefully consider the lighting situation and adjust the white balance accordingly. Remember, when you white-balance, you are telling the camera what type of light to expect. To get a feel for this concept, place your camcorder on a tripod and make some videotape before white-balancing. Then, with the tape still running, white-balance the camera. The difference is quite dramatic. White balance is the first building block of good television production lighting.

Three-Point Lighting: The Foundation of All Lighting

Whether you're lighting a school news set or a network drama, the same basic concept of three-point lighting prevails. In three-point lighting, lighting instruments serve three basic functions: a key light, a fill light, and a backlight.

The key light is the main source of illumination for the subject of your shot. The key light should provide enough illumination by itself to enable the video camera to produce a video signal. The subject-key light distance will vary according to the strength of the light. The key light should be placed in front of and facing the subject, about 5 to 10 degrees off center. Unless you're trying to create some special lighting effects, the key light should be placed about eye-level to the subject.

Although the key light adequately illuminates the subject, it can cast sharp shadows across his or her face. These shadows are removed by the second light, the fill light. The fill light is placed off-camera and beside the subject. The fill light should be aimed so that it removes most of the shadow from the side of the face.

The subject should now be adequately illuminated and free from shadows. However, a strong shadow is probably thrown onto the background wall. That shadow is removed with a backlight. The backlight should be either placed on the floor or hung from the ceiling and aimed onto the background wall. This light should be strong enough to effectively eliminate the shadows caused by the key light. The backlight also serves to create distance between the subject and the background in the otherwise flat TV environment.

As we continue our brief section on lighting, remember the three-point lighting concept. Chances are most of your video production locations, whether they be a small news studio or an auditorium, have some existing light. Analyze that light. It can be categorized as fill light (like overhead fluorescent lights) or backlight (on an auditorium stage). Therefore, your job becomes one of enhancing the natural environmental light to produce a sharp television signal.

Lighting Instruments for Schools

Although professional lights can be quite expensive, other forms of light can be used in school television production. Hardware stores sell clamp lights—a light bulb socket with a reflector pan and a clamp for mounting—for less than $10. These instruments, when fitted with the recommended wattage household bulb, can provide effective key, fill, and backlight lighting. Because the reflector is usually aluminum in content, these lights can get very hot if left on for more than a few minutes. Safety is always the prime consideration when working with lighting.

Professional lighting instruments can be used effectively in school settings. Professional light kits, which sell for a few hundred dollars, usually consist of at least three lighting instruments, stands, and reflectors—in other words, all of the lighting instruments an elementary or middle school would ever need. Although the cost may seem high at the outset, such a purchase will probably serve the school video production department for many years.

Changing the Light with Gels and Scrims

If the light produced by your clamp lights or professional light instruments seems harsh, or you would like to add a slight tint to the light, you can purchase scrims or gels (fig. 1.21). Many companies manufacture and sell these specially synthetic sheets that can be trimmed and attached to your lighting instruments. Gel is a translucent, synthetic material that adds color to light. Although it appears to be just colored plastic, it can withstand the heat produced by most lighting instruments. Scrim is somewhat more opaque, and serves to diffuse harsh light. Scrim is often made

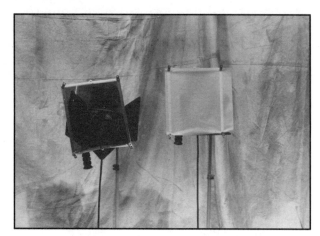

Fig. 1.21. Two lights: one with gel on the left, the other with scrim on the right.

from spun cloth, glass, or even fiberglass. Like gel, scrim can withstand the heat of studio lighting.

Nonstudio Lighting Applications

Lighting can also be manipulated to augment the natural light encountered when shooting outside "in the field." A battery-powered portable light can be attached to most camcorders to produce adequate illumination in low-light situations. You can purchase these portable video lights from most department stores that sell camcorders. They usually cost less than $100. If you will only use the light once or twice a year, renting is an option. Daily rental costs about $15 and should include a charged battery and a new bulb.

Videographers who find themselves shooting in bright, shadow-casting sunlight could probably use a homemade reflector board. Begin with a piece of white posterboard or foam-core board. Crinkle several large strips of aluminum foil and attach the foil to the board. Now you have a two-sided reflector board that can be used to focus sunlight onto the shadow of your subject's face; a student or fellow teacher can hold the board. The white side can be used when the light is very bright, and the aluminum side will amplify as well as reflect the light. The posterboard can be rolled or even folded for easy storage. Even though this concept sounds too easy, it really works. Try it, and you'll be hooked.

Remember, safety is always the prime consideration when using lighting instruments. Electricity and heat present a situation that requires twice as much caution. Always read instructions and use common sense. TV production should be fun, not painful!

Upgrading a Basic System

Perhaps most of your video production goals can be met with a simple video setup: a camcorder on a tripod with a microphone and possibly a lighting instrument. However, there will probably be times when you will want to give your productions a more professional look. At this point, you are ready to upgrade your system by adding more video equipment.

Upgrading your video system has three distinct benefits in the educational setting. First, the finished product looks more professional. A school play shot with a single camcorder will consist of a single still shot, annoying zooms, and tedious pans. However, by employing a video switcher, a second camera can shoot close-ups while the first camera remains on the group shot. Second, an expanded system gives the video producer more control over the situation. Let's use the example of the school play, this time adding an audio mixer. One microphone can be placed in front of the student singing group, a second microphone can be placed in the area of student activity, and a third microphone can be placed on the narrator's lectern. When all three microphones are connected to an audio mixer, the sound can be combined in the appropriate combinations, boosting or depleting each source. Finally, adding a few items of equipment creates educational opportunities for students to work in video production. Older students can learn to operate video switchers and audio mixers. Imagine the excitement on a fifth-grader's face upon learning that he or she has been chosen as the audio technician for the school play! This is an experience that simply cannot be duplicated in the classroom.

— 41 —
Upgrading a Basic System

Using video switchers and audio mixers means that you will not be using the camcorder to record the actual video. The camcorder (or camcorders) will provide the video signal, but the videotape will actually be recorded by a separate VCR. This VCR may be a standard unit that is checked out to classrooms on a daily basis. Or you may decide to use a higher-quality industrial VCR to do the job. Industrial VCRs are quite a bit more expensive than their consumer counterparts, but they offer higher-quality video recording, hi-fi sound, and adjustable stereo audio inputs. If you don't have a high-quality industrial VCR, you may want to add it to your "wish list." But don't worry: Everything discussed in this section can be recorded with a standard VCR.

Earlier in this chapter we studied such audio connectors as the ¼-inch phone jack, ⅛-inch mini jack, and the XLR connector. Now, we need to unveil three other types of connectors: phono (or RCA), BNC, and F-connector (or RF). A phono connector is a metal shaft surrounded by metal flanges that serve to secure the connector (fig. 1.22). The phono connector, commonly called the RCA connector after the company that developed it, is used in audio and video production. The BNC connec-

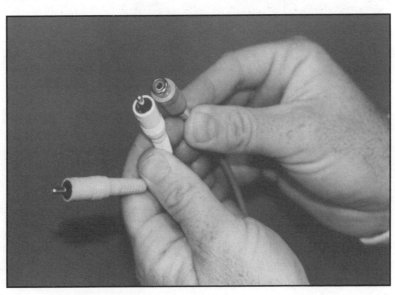

Fig. 1.22. Phono connector.

tor is similar to the phono connector except that the BNC uses a twist-lock mechanism to secure the connection (fig. 1.23). The BNC is quite popular when connecting video components. The F-connector is the thin, sharp copper wire that we use to connect VCRs to television sets (see fig. 1.24 on page 42). Take a few minutes to examine your VCR inputs and outputs and determine what kind of connectors you have. Knowing what you have will become important as we discuss audio and video system connections in greater detail.

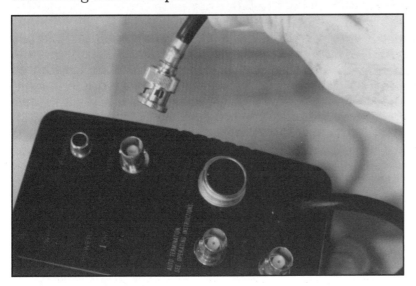

Fig. 1.23. BNC connector.

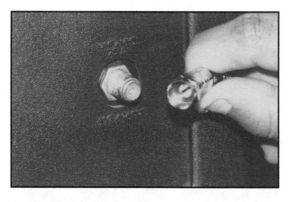

Fig. 1.24. F-connector.

Switchers and Special Effects Generators

Upgrading the video signal in television production means connecting two or more video sources (video camera, camcorders, or VCRs) to a switcher or special effects generator, which in turn relays the signal to the input of your recording VCR.

The Switcher

In its simplest form, a video switcher allows the videographer to select one video source from the video sources that have been connected. This selection is usually made by pressing a button on a single row of buttons. Suppose two cameras are connected to a simple video switcher. Pressing the button marked "1" would send the signal from camera 1 to the VCR. Pressing the button marked "2" would send the signal from camera 2 to the VCR. This simple, total selection is called a video "cut."

The Special Effects Generator (SEG)

Cutting from camera 1 to camera 2 may be just fine for some video productions. However, to perform more complex transitions from camera 1 to camera 2 you will need a special effects generator, or SEG. An SEG can perform simple video cuts, just like the switcher. But it can also manipulate the video signal in other ways. To accomplish more complex transitions, an SEG has two or more busses, or rows, of selection buttons. A fader bar is located between each pair of busses. Therefore, an SEG with two busses will have a single fader bar. An SEG with three busses will have two fader bars, and so on. Let's walk through a simple dissolve from camera 1 to camera 2 on an SEG. In a dissolve, the original signal fades out as the new signal fades in. On the top bus (row of buttons), we select "camera 1." On the second (lower) bus, we select "camera 2." By moving the fader bar from the top bus position to the lower bus position, we perform the dissolve transition.

Other transitions commonly found on SEGs are fades and wipes. A fade is a dissolve to a background color. Instead of dissolving from camera 1 to camera 2, we may choose to fade from camera 1 to "black." (Most special effects generators produce background colors and offer them as a bus selection.) In a wipe, one video image seems to push another video image off the screen. SEGs are often programmed to produce a large number of wipes. The most common wipes are vertical and horizontal. More expensive SEGs usually offer more wipe patterns. A wipe is usually performed by selecting the first video source in the top bus, selecting the second video source in the second bus, and pushing a button on the SEG that selects the desired wipe pattern. Then, as the fader bar is moved from the first bus to the second bus, the wipe is performed on the screen.

Time-Base Corrector

Some video switchers and special effects generators require the use of a special piece of equipment for each switcher input. This item of equipment is called a time-base corrector (TBC). A time-base corrector takes an inherently unstable video signal and converts it into a rock-solid signal. This solid, corrected signal is necessary for combining signals from video sources. Generally, when a VCR is introduced into the switching equation, a TBC must be used. Fortunately, video manufacturers have recognized this need and responded in two ways: (1) by creating switchers and SEGs that don't need time-base correction, and (2) by making a built-in TBC a feature of their newer VCRs. Make sure to investigate TBC problems before purchasing equipment for your school. SEGs that have a bargain price attached may require expensive additional equipment for successful connection and operation.

Passing Lines of Resolution

As we stated before, a switcher or SEG takes in a video signal from one of several sources (cameras, VCRs), manipulates it, and sends it to a VCR for recording. A good switcher/SEG will maintain the quality of the video signal as it processes it. Here's an example. Imagine that you have connected two camcorders to an SEG, and you're recording the output on a standard VHS videotape. A VHS tape, performing under optimum conditions, can pass about 240 lines of resolution. This is a measure of the maximum quality of the picture. A medium-quality camcorder can produce well over 300 lines of resolution. You want to use a switcher that will have the capacity to process at least 240 of those lines for recording. Some cheaper SEGs will pass only 150-200 lines, causing significant loss of picture quality. Make sure that the switcher/SEG is not a weak link in your video chain.

Video Signal and RF Signal

In our example above, we connected the outputs of two camcorders to an SEG. The SEG processed the signal (allowing us to perform cuts, fades, dissolves, etc.) and sent the result to a VCR for recording. This entire process was completed using *video* signals. A video signal is produced by video cameras/camcorders, and is processed by switchers and SEGs.

Examine the outputs of a standard consumer VCR, and the input of a television set. This connection uses an RF signal. RF (the abbreviation for radio frequency) contains both the audio and video signals. Further examination of the outputs of the VCR will probably yield another set of jacks. These will be labeled (or similarly labeled) "video-out," "video-in," "audio-out," and "audio-in." These are inputs and outputs for audio and video signals, not RFs. Therefore, when connecting switchers and SEGs to VCRs (used as inputs *or* outputs) use the "video" signals. The RF signal is reserved for connection of the VCR to a television for viewing of the final project as it is being recorded.

Audio Mixers and Music Sources

Just as an SEG allows for the combination and selection of video sources, an audio mixer allows for the combination and selection of different audio sources. With an audio mixer you can connect several audio inputs, such as microphones, music sources, and even sound from a VCR (see fig. 1.25 on page 44).

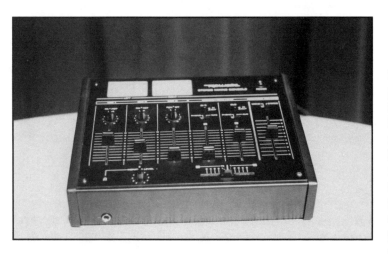

Fig. 1.25. Audio mixer.

Microphones

Most audio mixers feature three or more microphone inputs. Imagine you are celebrating Intellectual Freedom Week at your elementary school, and you have assembled a group of three children's book authors to present a panel discussion for the media center advisory council. Because you anticipate a great discussion, you decide to videotape it (after obtaining the authors' permission) using a full complement of audio and video equipment. Each panel member would wear a lavaliere microphone, and the moderator would use a desk microphone mounted on the lectern. Therefore, you would need four microphone inputs on your audio mixer. Again, don't forget to match the microphone impedance to the audio mixer impedance (Hi-Z or Low-Z), or purchase impedance line adapters.

Music Sources

So that this will be a classy production, you decide to include a few seconds of production music (copyright-cleared) at the beginning of your program. The source for this music, whether it be an audiocassette deck or a compact disc player, must be connected to an input of the audio mixer. This input may be labeled "cassette" or "aux," or perhaps even "line-in."

You also plan to incorporate into your production a brief video that has been prepared in advance. In the video, elementary students hold examples of banned children's books and say the title and the author. You plan to use this tape in your panel discussion program. Therefore the audio output of the VCR that will play this brief program must also be connected to the audio mixer. Once again, use a "line-in" input of the audio mixer. The output of the audio mixer must then be connected to the input of the *recording* VCR.

Let's review the audio connections: The four microphones—one for each guest and one for the moderator—are connected to the microphone inputs on the audio mixer. The music source—cassette or CD—is connected to a "line" input of the audio mixer. The sound from your source VCR (with the student segment) is connected to a different "line" input. Finally, the output of the audio mixer is connected to the input of the VCR to be recorded, simultaneously with video signal, on videotape.

Adjusting the Audio Mixer

Audio mixers feature dials or fader bars that allow a technician to adjust sound levels to create an evenly mixed audio signal. The audio technician uses VU meters as tools for proper adjustment. A VU (volume unit) meter can be either analog or LED. Both meters serve the same function. The total audio signal should approach the "red" markings on the meter, but not regularly go into the red (fig. 1.26).

The border between "safe" and "red" represents 100 percent. If the needle or LED is frequently in the red, distortion is likely to occur, and the audio signal recorded on the VCR will be muddy and overmodulated.

Remember that the audio signals in an audio mixer are additive. In other words, they compound upon one another. If microphone #1 is currently measuring about 75 percent, and the speaker using microphone #2 interrupts and begins

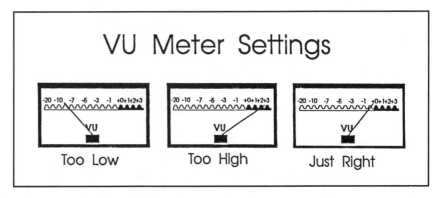

Fig. 1.26. VU meter adjustments.

talking at the same time, the meter will go well into the red. Quickly adjust the inputs so that the total VU is near 100 percent.

Audio/Video Mixers

Fig. 1.27. A/V mixer.

Realizing the need in the market for audio-visual systems that are compact and relatively easy to operate, some manufacturers have created A/V mixers that combine audio and video functions into a single item of equipment. These systems frequently allow for connection of two or three video sources, and two or three audio sources (fig. 1.27). Some A/V mixers also have special digital effects, such as strobe, still-frame, and paintbox. They may also use technology that eliminates the need for time-base correction (see fig. 1.28 on page 46).

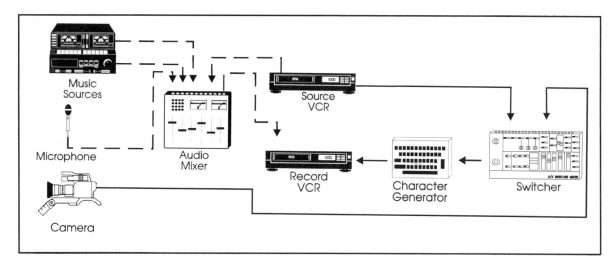

Fig. 1.28. Audio/video connections.

Graphics

Graphics can make your programs look more sophisticated and professional. A simple title for your program, or a "name tag" for your announcement show host, can add that extra element that will make your audience sit up and take notice. Graphics can also provide additional information for your program. Adding a graphic to announce the time and place of the PTA meeting on your announcement show will help students remember to tell their parents. And if you've been assigned the task of videotaping the principal's opening address to the school, a simple graphic can help the audience visualize and remember the principal's three goals for the school year. Graphics production, with or without professional equipment, can also be fun, providing an artistic and creative outlet for your students. The simple exercise of reading characters on the screen will help struggling readers in both elementary and middle schools understand the relationship between these referents and the words they represent. Whether the students are creating the graphics, or reading them from the TV screen, they can make the programs more informative, understandable, and enjoyable.

Guidelines for Graphics

Before we cover specific techniques of graphic preparation and presentation, let's look at the three basic guidelines for graphic creation: color, size, and time.

Color

Most graphics incorporate color. Colors can help set the mood or tone of your presentation. Bright colors can also add energy to your presentation. But probably the most important aspect of color involves choosing colors that provide a high contrast on the television screen. For example, yellow letters on a white background will probably not show up very well on the television screen, and like it or not, most video cameras have trouble with at least one of the primary colors of television. Graphics production for video provides an excellent opportunity to teach about the primary colors. Now the old "color wheel" takes on new meaning, as students select contrasting colors that will appear bright and brilliant on the television screen. Teachers also have the opportunity to teach the difference between the subtractive primary colors used in painting (red, blue, and *yellow*) and the additive primary colors used in television production (red, blue, and *green*). Finally, graphics should always be checked for color contrast on a monochrome (black-and-white) television as well as a color television. The absence of color ensures that *brightness*, the essential element of contrast, will be emphasized; the readability of your graphics on a black-and-white television ensures that audience members who are color-blind can read them as well.

Size

Although color is important to graphics production, the prime objective of the process is to provide a readable message; the size of the letters on the television screen is crucial to meeting this objective. There is no magic formula to calculate the size of the graphics needed. The key consideration is your audience. Under what conditions will *they* be watching the program? The optimal condition has the viewer no farther in *feet* than the width of the screen in *inches*. For example, students watching a 20-inch television should be no farther than 20 feet from the screen. However, the screen-audience distance is meaningless when the graphics are too small to read. The problem of "too small graphics" is twofold. First, the creator always has a good view of the graphic because he or she is usually at arm's length. Whether the creator is drawing on art paper or working on a character generator, he or she is usually no more than a few inches from the graphic. The solution: Videotape the graphic, and watch it at the same distance as your audience. Second, there is a tendency to put too much information on the screen. The solution: Establish size and number-of-words standards for your presentations. Remember, you can always go to another screen. If your video has five different messages to show the audience, consider using five different screens instead of cramming all of the information onto one screen. Teaching students to follow these standards will help them learn about visual literacy and spatial relationships. Big graphics have impact. A series of sentences printed on a single screen presents the viewer with a difficult task and takes much of the enjoyment out of viewing the program.

Time

Make sure that each graphic is displayed for an adequate amount of time. How much time is enough? Use this yardstick: The viewer should be able to read the graphic aloud slowly while it is on the screen. Of course, the reading ability of your audience must be considered. New readers will need more time on each page.

If you are using a camcorder, check the manual or experiment to determine the start-up and rollback time of the equipment. When you push the trigger to *start* recording on your camcorder, how much time elapses until actual recording begins? When you push the trigger to *stop* recording, how far does the tape "roll back"? This time is usually about one second. If you decide that your graphic should be displayed for five seconds, you may have to allow almost twice as much time between trigger pushes. Remember: Experiment with your equipment to avoid graphics "flashes." Subliminal messages are highly unethical!

Creating Graphics Without a Character Generator

A character generator is a video component that allows a technician to type words and symbols onto the television screen. Character generators often include various fonts (type styles) and character sizes. Some character generators also allow for storage of graphics pages in RAM memory or on computer disks.

As you can probably guess, most character generators are expensive. Basic models start at about $500. Other models are less expensive but they sacrifice quality for cost. Media specialists who can spend an hour or two with a group of students can teach the basic skills of electronic character generation.

Fortunately, great graphics can be made without a character generator. A "low-tech/high-touch" approach will save money and headaches while allowing all students to creatively contribute to your school programs. Let's look at some techniques for making great graphics without a character generator.

Hand-Drawn Graphics

This is the most obvious, and probably one of the most creative, techniques for making graphics without a character generator. By using a special feature included in your camcorder, you can make your hand-drawn graphics as small as a notecard. Most video cameras and camcorders have a macro lens—a special lens installed within the camera's zoom lens that allows the camera operator to fill the screen with a very small object. A coin, a photograph, or a postage stamp can be videotaped in this manner. Accessing your camera's macro lens usually involves pushing a button near the front of the lens. (Consult your camera's manual for specific instructions.) Students can create their graphics on note-cards or drawing paper, then videotape them using the camcorder and a tripod. When creating these graphics don't stop with crayons on white paper. Use bright posterboard, glitter pens, and foil stars to add color and excitement. One teacher went to a hardware store, where the manager was happy to donate small wallpaper samples to use for graphics creation. Wood scraps and material remnants can also make great backgrounds.

When creating hand-drawn graphics, it is important to understand and remember the *aspect ratio* of television production. The aspect ratio refers to the relationships between the height and width of the television screen. In television production, the aspect ratio is 3 x 4. This means that the television picture is three units tall and four units wide. Exceeding this aspect ratio requires cutting off part of the picture. Remember, this is a ratio, not a measurement. Imagine that your students are making graphics for your school news show opening. Your paper is 9 inches high. How long should it be? Using the 3 x 4 aspect ratio, you should cut the paper to measure 9 inches by 12 inches. Notecards that measure 3 inches by 5 inches must be trimmed an inch to meet this ratio. Hand-drawn graphics are fun for all age groups. They can be used for show openings, lunch menus, and any number of school announcements. "Today's graphics were created by Ms. Nelson's eighth-grade art class" will heighten interest in your program, and give your audience another reason to watch attentively.

Placecards

Hand-drawn graphics work well for full-screen shots. But if your dream is to display your students' names when they are reading announcements, you need to use another technique. You can make giant placecards using cardboard and contrasting lettering. Lettering can be produced using professional lettering machines (such as Letteron) or purchased from most office supply stores. Sticky-backed plastic letters are quite easy to use. Rub-off letters are less expensive, but more difficult to use. Make sure to follow the guidelines of size and contrast discussed earlier. Once you have mounted the letters on cardboard, mount the placecards on your news desk using tape or sticky tack.

Large Letters

Use bulletin board letters—machine or handmade—to display your show's name on the background behind your news readers. Tape the letters to the wall or curtain that serves as your background. These letters can be changed frequently to keep your background fresh and interesting.

Glass Painting

Let's say you're making a school orientation program, and you want to begin with a shot of the school exterior with the school name along the bottom of the shot. Using paint or plastic letters, create the title on a pane of glass and shoot the scene while an assistant holds the glass in the correct position in front of the camera. Of course, use caution while working with elementary students and glass!

Letter Boards

Most office supply stores sell letter boards with white plastic letters and a grooved black background. (If you've ever been to a deli, you know what we're talking about. In fact, a parent who works as a soda or beer distributor may be able to donate one of these.) Arrange your letters and shoot a close-up or macro of the graphic. Although this approach may not be as creative or visually appealing as hand-drawn graphics, it is quick, easy to read, and simple for students to create.

Computer Screens and Printers

Many educational and utility computer programs provide onscreen graphics or printouts suitable for program use. When videotaping a computer screen, turn out all the lights and connect your camcorder to an external monitor to make any fine-tuning adjustments. Banner and bookmark programs may be especially suited for printout graphics. Don't forget the aspect ratio.

Objects

Several objects found in elementary school classrooms can be used to create graphics. Building blocks can spell out your show title. Any alphabet teaching tool can be recombined to spell a graphic. Creative middle school students can find several objects around campus to spell out the name of the daily news show.

Creative Display

Even though it might be easiest to simply shoot many of these graphics with a camera on a tripod, at least experiment with different ways of presentation. Staging several scenes around campus can make your graphics more entertaining and communicative. Tape the graphic to a lunch tray, and when a student lifts his plate, the graphic appears. Tape the graphic to a teacher's grade book. When the teacher opens the grade book, zoom in on the graphic. Tape the graphic to a bookmark, and when the student opens the book, the graphic appears (try an over-the-shoulder shot). Or students can finger paint graphics while the camera rolls. Many camcorders feature simple stop action animation in which the camcorder records a few frames at a time. Be creative. Make each letter appear individually, or animate building blocks moving across the screen. This form of presentation will make your graphics come alive for your students.

Making graphics without a character generator is a fun, creative process that involves students in every grade level. Students will be excited to see their artistic creations used as titles for the news show, and students too small or young to operate video equipment or read announcements can have an active part in the show. Although these techniques may seem primitive, they offer better results and more flexibility than low-end character generators and provide valuable educational opportunities.

Creating Graphics Using a Character Generator

Perhaps you are considering the purchase of a professional character generator. If you produce a daily news show, or provide a large number of in-house video services, a stand-alone character generator (CG) system will help make your programs more watchable, effective, and educational. In this section, we will look at moderately priced CG systems, the concept of connecting a CG to your existing video production system, and criteria for selection.

What's Out There

Just as many different types of VCRs are available on the market, there are many different CG systems with *very* different prices. Character generators used by television networks can cost $100,000 or more. However, there are several excellent CGs that would work well on the elementary or middle school level that can be purchased for a few hundred dollars. They include camera-based, A/V mixer-based, computer-based, and stand-alone CGs.

Camera-Based Character Generators. Some video cameras and camcorders have built-in character generators, or offer small character generators as an optional accessory (fig. 1.29). These camera-based systems usually offer the user four or five lines of graphics. Some systems also offer storage of a few pages of graphics. More advanced camera-based systems allow the videographer to scroll and crawl the pages. These graphics can usually be superimposed over video or solid background colors generated by the camera. The downside of camera-based graphics is that its small size makes creating graphics a relatively tedious operation. Frequently the buttons are so small that a metal "toothpick" must be used for typing. Camera-based CGs also offer only one font (type style) and character size. Still, camera-based graphics offer a foot in the door of the graphics market and

Fig. 1.29. Camera-based character generator.

cost relatively little. A camera-based character generator represents a good investment to schools doing a very limited amount of video production.

A/V Mixer-Based Character Generators. Many A/V mixers—the stand-alone audio and video mixing systems—also include an optional character generator that can be attached to the mixer via a special port on the mixer. An A/V mixer-based CG is a nice entry-level accessory for schools producing video programs on a regular basis. These CGs usually include moderate-quality graphics, multiple-page storage, and perhaps an optional font.

Computer-Based Character Generators. Video production professionals are recognizing increasingly the value of interfacing powerful personal computers with video equipment. Graphic, paint-box, and animation functions were the first to build the bridge between the computer and video production. Computer hardware companies have designed and manufactured components that transfer the VGA computer signal into video and RF signals. If you have access to the appropriate hardware and can budget the software purchase, you may want to consider implementing this system. In any case, you will need to consult with a computer specialist to determine the compatibility of this expensive software with your existing video equipment.

Stand-Alone Character Generators. Full-sized character generators are really computers programmed to produce professional graphics for your television production system (fig. 1.30).

Stand-alone systems range in price from about $500 to the thousands of dollars spent by television networks. Stand-alone systems offer multiple fonts and colors, character sizes, underlining, and long-term storage of many pages of graphics. Well-funded elementary and middle schools are making eye-catching graphics with new character generators that combine simplistic operation and high-tech results.

Fig. 1.30. Stand-alone character generator. Photo courtesy of Videonics.

If you are involved in intensive video production for your school and community, you should consider the purchase of such a system when budget or grant money becomes available.

Connecting a Character Generator to Your Video System

There are many ways to connect a character generator to your existing video setup. The best bet is to get this information from the vendor *before* making the purchase, but we'll also provide a brief explanation here.

The character generator needs to be connected between the switcher/SEG output and the recording VCR. If you're using a camera-based system, this is already done for you—the characters are added to the video signal before the signal is passed on to the recorder. With a CG designed for use as a component of an A/V mixer system, the connection is usually made using a port on the A/V mixer. Adding graphics is usually a matter of pushing a button on the A/V mixer to call up the graphics. Computer and stand-alone CGs are a little trickier. If your video switcher has an extra input, you can connect the CG system as a switcher input and simply switch to graphics or overlay using the fader bar when needed. If an extra input is not available, you must connect the CG in between the switcher and recording VCR. This technique is known as Down-Stream Key. The output of the switcher is connected to the input of the character generator. The signal passes through the character generator, giving the CG the chance to add any necessary graphics. The CG output, which now consists of the switcher output *and* graphics, is then sent to the VCR for recording. Most stand-alone CGs have a "transparent" background choice, which allows the graphics to be keyed (placed) over the video processed by the switcher, as well as solid background colors. When operating a stand-alone character generator, the system must have a separate monitor for the "preview" output of the CG. This preview displays the signal before it is sent to the recording VCR. Once again, however, consult with the vendor to ensure the compatibility of all equipment *before* purchase.

Criteria for Character Generator Selection

As we stated earlier, there is a tremendous range of quality in the character generator market. Here are some of the most important criteria for selecting any character generation system, from camera-based to stand-alone.

Character Appearance. This is the most important feature of any character generation system. The characters should be well formed, easy to read, and professional in appearance. Some less expensive CGs offer only dot-matrix graphics that resemble the "draft" setting on a 24-pin computer printer. Others are, of course, professional quality (fig. 1.31).

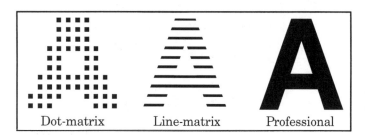

Dot-matrix   Line-matrix   Professional

Fonts. The font is the type style of the character. Will the CG type in several different styles, or are you restricted to a single font? Underlining and boldfacing abilities should also be considered.

Fig. 1.31. Varying character quality.

Character Size. Is the technician able to select from a variety of character sizes? Many less expensive systems offer only one size of text.

Colors. A good character generator should offer several colors for the letters and the backgrounds. Also, the transparent background should be available if you want to put graphics over a video image produced by a camera or VCR.

Ease of Use. Even though a character generator is a complex device, it should be very user-friendly. Consider the complexity of the commands and the procedure for changing pages. How many buttons need to be pushed in order to change the colors or character size? Because graphics frequently need to be changed as a program is being produced, graphic entry should be simple and direct.

Pages of Working Memory. A CG should allow an adequate number of pages (at least a dozen) to be saved in working memory.

Page Storage and Retrieval. Many stand-alone CGs have computer floppy disk drives that enable storage of an infinite number of computer pages. This feature could come in handy for extended projects or multiple-user situations. Less expensive systems offer storage on an internal chip powered by a long-life battery. Try to imagine situations in which you would use the same graphics on several different shoots. A storage/retrieval system can eliminate the need to reenter the same graphics for each production.

Crawl/Scroll. A "crawl" is a movement of characters across the screen, usually from right to left. Crawls are used frequently in TV news to inform the public of "special bulletins." A "scroll" is a bottom-to-top movement of characters and is frequently found in ending credits. Not all CGs perform these tasks. Also, inspect the character appearance during a scroll or crawl. Some characters that look great on graphics screens become shaky and unreadable during crawls and scrolls.

Inputs and Outputs. Make sure that the CG will connect appropriately to your system. The preview monitor output is very important if you wish to create new graphics during a program's production.

Carefully evaluate your needs before you decide to purchase an expensive character generator. Consult with your district office, and see what graphics services they can offer. If you will only need complex electronic graphics once or twice a year, you can probably get by using the physical graphics described earlier in this section, a camera-based system for electronic character generation, and the professional graphics services of your district office for those special video projects.

Equipment Security

Every year we hear about one or two schools in our area who have lost their video equipment to theft. When thieves break into a school, they usually head straight for the video equipment because of its high value. As the popularity of consumer electronics increases, so will the demand for stolen electronics. In a time when popularity is determined not by knowledge but by the volume of a stereo and the quality of a VCR, thieves will walk past an entire row of fully equipped computers to steal one camcorder.

Obviously, it is important to store all items of audio and video equipment in locked areas. The wisest course of action is to determine the room most isolated by locks and solid doors, and store your video equipment there. A thief should never be able to smash a single window or pick a single lock to steal video equipment. In the quest for the order dictated by cataloging and book arranging, media specialists often make the mistake of putting the sign "TV Production Storage Room" on the door. Really, no one except the media center staff should even know where the room is.

It is also important to reinforce any locked cabinets in which equipment is stored. Prefer locked cabinets over the storage of equipment on metal shelving. If you feel that the cabinets could be compromised by a crowbar, ask the school custodial personnel to add an extra lock. Keep a key on your key ring, and give the spare to your principal. Do not simply place the key in your desk. That is the first place a thief will look upon breaking in. From our experience, most media center thefts are of the "smash and grab" variety. One or two extra security locks may help deter after-hours theft, especially if the thieves are people who have easily gained access to the school building.

Another reason for adding locks is for insurance purposes. Most property insurance will pay only for thefts that result from forced entry. Even if the thieves are successful in their primary task, their violation of your additional lock will help determine that forced entry was indeed involved. One school recently opened an audio/video equipment storage room and found it empty! Thousands of dollars of audio/video equipment had been stolen with no sign of forced entry. An extra lock—this one smashed by the thieves—would have helped the school make a successful insurance claim.

Daytime access to equipment should also be restricted. It is not wise to allow students, faculty, and staff members to wander through the television production studio or the storage room. Only media center personnel and your selected students should be allowed unescorted entry. A wireless microphone system costing hundreds of dollars could easily be put in a pocket. Such a theft could represent the loss of the entire year's video production budget.

Make a habit of keeping track of your video production equipment. Some television production instructors mentally itemize all equipment on a daily basis. If each item of equipment has a specified place in a storage cabinet, a quick glance will let you know if there are any missing items.

Entire video production departments have been decimated by theft. Even if the losses are covered by insurance, replacement can take months and the policy may pay only a depreciated value, which will prohibit true replacement of the equipment. Take care of your school's investment in television production.

Picture Composition

This chapter, by far the longest in the book, has been designed as a primer on video production equipment. We have discussed in full just about every piece of production equipment that an elementary or middle school media center would own. What we cannot do is give you experience with the equipment—that is up to you. However, at this point we would like to offer a few tips about picture composition. Because television is definitely a visual medium, it is hard to describe the concepts of picture composition on a printed page. We'll try, though, and if you would like a complete visual reference, consider viewing the last 15 minutes of the videotape companion to our first book, *Television Production: A Classroom Approach.* The picture composition recommendations listed here are part of the dozen "Video Tips" found on the videotape.

The Rule of Thirds

The rule of thirds states that in most video production, the exciting parts of the shot should be along a third of the screen, not centered. Imagine drawing a tic-tac-toe grid on the television screen. What you have actually done is divide the screen into thirds, both vertically and horizontally. There are four intersections of those lines. The rule of thirds says that the subject(s) of your shot should be positioned on those lines, and the most interesting part of your shot should be on the intersections of the lines (fig. 1.32).

For example, imagine that you are videotaping a first-grade student painting in art class for a school orientation video. You "could" shoot from the front with the child centered in the shot. Using the rule of thirds would have the shot taken from a side angle, with the child lined up on one third and her paintbrush crossing the center onto the paper, which is positioned on the other third. This makes the shot much more visually appealing (figs. 1.33 and 1.34).

Foreground, Middle Ground, and Background

Another rule involves the number 3. Give your video shots depth by using foreground, middle ground, and background in each shot. Don't shoot "flat" shots that are hard to watch. For example, in the same video, let's say you are featuring the media center's book collection. A simple shot would be to stand in front of the bookshelf and roll tape (fig. 1.35 on page 56). A better shot using the rule stated above would be to shoot the bookshelf from a 45-degree angle, creating a diagonal across the screen (fig. 1.36 on page 56). Then, have a student approach the shelf and pull a book from it. A media specialist could approach from behind and talk to the student about the book. This shot employs foreground, middle ground,

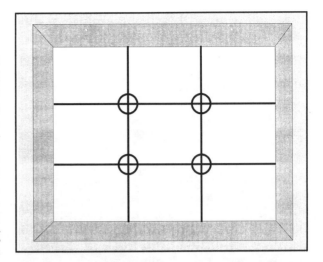

Fig. 1.32. Rule of thirds. © Mark Volpe, 1993

Fig. 1.33. Rule of thirds "before."

Fig. 1.34. Rule of thirds "after."

and background. Not all of your shots can include all three. But try to make your shots work on at least two levels.

Fig. 1.35. Flat shot.

Fig. 1.36. Shot corrected.

Headroom

Every person in your shot needs a small but comfortable amount of room between the top of the head and the top of the television screen. This concept is known as headroom. Using too little headroom will give the appearance of the head rubbing against the top frame of the screen. Using too much headroom centers the head in the shot, making the person seem very small, almost as if he or she is standing on tiptoes to even see into the shot.

In both the elementary and middle school settings, you will probably be interviewing people of very different heights; for example, your principal may be 3 feet taller than some of the students. For this reason, it is important to find the proper level of your shot. A basic rule to follow is this: Everyone involved in the video shot should be at the same level. If you are conducting an interview on camera, the videographer, the interviewer, and the guest should all be on the same level, whether it is seated, standing, or a combination of both, based on height (fig. 1.37). The concept of finding the proper level for the shot also applies to basic school videography. Imagine that you are including a shot of the principal sitting at her desk in your school orientation video. The common approach would be for the videographer to stand in front of the desk for the shot. But this would produce a downward angle that would make an uncomfortable, demeaning shot. Instead, the videographer could sit in front of the desk and videotape an even-level shot of the principal at her desk.

Fig. 1.37. Elementary student interviewing the school principal.

Noseroom/Leadroom

A concept similar to headroom in videography is noseroom/leadroom. Noseroom is the amount of space left on the video screen in front of the subject when the subject is shot in profile. Leadroom is the amount of room in front of a subject who is walking or running. Using the proper amount of noseroom, someone seated in profile should have at least half of the screen "in front of his or her nose." As the degree of profile decreases, the amount of noseroom also decreases. Set up an imaginary angle for the person shot in profile. That angle would be 90 degrees—the measurement in degrees from the camera lens to the nose of the subject. As the degree measure decreases, the amount of noseroom should decrease accordingly.

When a subject is walking or running through the shot, the concept of noseroom is translated to leadroom—the amount of space in between the moving subject and the edge of the screen. The videographer should try to lead the subject into the shot, rather than follow him or her through it. For example, in a shot of a basketball player dribbling down the court from right to left, we should see the player on the right-hand part of the screen; the rest of the picture should be reserved for the player's teammates and opponents. Here's another example: Imagine that you plan to show in your school orientation tape a happy group of students leaving the bus loading area and entering the school building. For the sake of example, imagine that their walk is from left to right. The student group should appear on the left part of the screen, allowing the school door to come into the shot as early as possible. The videographer leads the students into the school. The alternative would be to center the student group, which would obscure the background and eliminate the concept of motion, or to follow the students, which would probably confuse the viewer.

Walk, Don't Zoom

The final composition concept offered involves the use of a zoom lens. Almost all camcorders are equipped with a zoom lens that allows the videographer to get a good close-up from across a crowded room. The side effect from zooming in all the way to get that close-up is a shaky shot. The zoom lens, when zoomed in all the way, will magnify even the slightest camera movement. The rule for videography is walk, don't zoom. If you plan to include students working at learning centers as part of your school orientation tape, walk up to the students and videotape the close-ups with the lens zoomed out all the way. This approach will minimize the effects of any camera movements caused by breathing, etc. The opposite approach, that of the "lazy camera operator," would be to stand in one spot in the room and shoot all of the activities taking place. This leads to a "home movie" look. Don't just pan, looking for a good shot with the camera rolling. Find a good close-up and walk to the shot.

In the previous few paragraphs, we have barely scratched the surface of good videography. If you're interested in developing advanced videography skills, we suggest our middle/high school text, *Television Production: A Classroom Approach.* Another suggestion is to watch videotapes that you like—movies, instructional shows, documentaries, etc.—and try to determine exactly what is visually appealing about these shows. Chances are they follow the same basic principles discussed here. Pick up your camcorder and make at least 30 minutes of tape every day. Examine the tape. Determine which shots work best. Additional reading, observation of working professionals, and firsthand experience are the keys to becoming a complete videographer.

Conclusion

Knowledge of the audio/video equipment that your school currently owns, as well as the availability of affordable equipment in the marketplace, will help you establish video production as a dynamic service in your elementary or middle school. There is certainly no substitute for expertise in this area. Your leadership in evaluating and selecting equipment will determine the instructional effectiveness of television production in your school.

2 NEWS SHOW CREATION AND CONTENT

An increasing number of schools are adding closed-circuit television systems to their school facility to show cable, broadcast, and videotaped programs to students and to conduct the daily school announcements, among other things. Most new elementary and middle schools are built with this in-house distribution system as part of the school communications installation. Television has taken a place alongside the chalkboard and overhead projector as a standard item of instructional equipment.

The task of supervising this system often falls on the shoulders of the media specialist. Included in this task is the responsibility of creating and supervising the production of a daily announcement program. This creates yet another highly visible responsibility for the media specialist. Yet production of a news show also offers the media specialist the opportunity to serve and promote the objectives of the school through the use of the media center. In this chapter, we will explore the complex task of producing a daily announcement show.

Guidelines and Philosophies

As with any organization, a daily announcement program needs a set of philosophies and guidelines to govern production activities. This may sound a bit formal for your announcement show, but establishing objectives can make your program more professional and allow for the teaching of important media skills.

Philosophies

Here are some philosophies to consider when deciding what kind of program you would like to produce with your students.

- Promote the positive attributes of your school. Solicit and announce the names of outstanding students and achievements. Recognize student awards and contributions to the school.

- Seek to improve student morale. School activity is a major source of pride and self-esteem for both elementary and middle school students. Recognition of student achievement can improve conduct and strengthen pride in the school.

- See your program as a service to the school and community. Don't be satisfied to wallow in the mire of lunchroom menus and tardiness warnings. Make your program a positive force in the school.

- Allow students to create as much of the program as possible. Most older elementary students can do more than sit in front of a camera and read lunch menus.

- Establish instructional, as well as communication, objectives. Set aside a few minutes each day to teach or reinforce a video skill.

- Emphasize the skills and benefits of working as a group. These skills transfer to many different areas of a child's education.

Guidelines

While philosophies will serve as the overriding principles of your television production program, guidelines will help in the daily operation of your news show. Here are some guidelines to consider.

- Establish a designated time and place for your program production. You may have a television production studio as part of the school facility. If not, you may need to use a nearby classroom, or a corner of the media center. Most daily shows are produced in the morning, but programs can also be prerecorded the afternoon before broadcast.

- Make the decision—live or tape. In order to save time, many schools put the students in front of the camera and begin the live program. Although videotaping for later broadcast may take more time, it has its benefits—most notably the ability to make simple edits and save students embarrassment if they make mistakes. If you decide to produce a more complex program including videotaped segments, taping is recommended.

- Decide on a format for your show. List all of the items to appear on your program and present them in a consistent order.

- Establish professional behavior guidelines. Some students may be prone to expressions of disgust when team members make mistakes. Use the opportunity to plant the seeds of professional conduct and maturity.

- Plan ahead for special events. Most students, for example, would love to see highlights from field day on the announcement program.

Types of News Shows

How you will apply the material in this chapter depends greatly on the type of news show that you wish to create. For the sake of simplicity, we will define these types as (1) the camcorder program, (2) the segment roll-in program, (3) the complete studio program, and (4) the magazine format.

The Camcorder Program

Equipment needed: Camcorder, microphone, tripod

The camcorder program is the simplest form of school news show to produce. The camcorder is placed on a tripod, and the student reader sits at a desk or table and reads the announcements. A desk or lavaliere microphone is connected to the camcorder to effectively pick up the audio. The output of the camcorder is connected directly to the distribution system for a live program, or a videotape is made in the camcorder for broadcast later.

Even though this announcement program is quite simple, it can be very effective. Students can use bulletin board paper, plants, and school-oriented items to decorate the set. You can use the camcorder's fade button to fade the picture in and out. The camcorder program is a good format for beginning television production students and media specialists.

The Segment Roll-In Program

Equipment needed: Camcorder, tripod, microphone, VCR(s)

As we've said, students enjoy seeing school activities on announcement programs. You can record and broadcast such activities by using an extra VCR. The connections are made in the same manner as for "the camcorder program" described above with the addition of a VCR to play segments. The video output of the camcorder is connected to the "video-in" jack on the VCR. The audio output of the camcorder is connected to the "audio-in" jack on the VCR. The outputs (audio and video) of this "segment" VCR are connected to the distribution system for live shows, or to the inputs of a second VCR for recording a program to be shown later (fig. 2.1). To play a segment, simply insert the segment videotape into the segment VCR and push "play." The tape in the VCR will override the audio

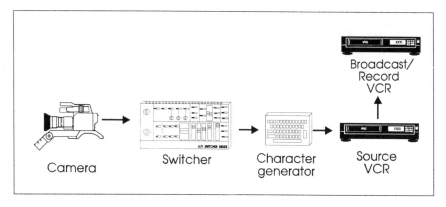

Fig. 2.1. Segment roll-in show.

and video from the camcorder. After the segment is finished, press the "stop" button, and the output will return to the camcorder audio and video. By adding a simple VCR to your television production system, you can make the announcement program much more enjoyable and informative.

The Complete Studio Program

Equipment needed: Camcorder, tripod, microphones, audio mixer, one or two VCRs, character generator (optional), second camcorder and video switcher (optional), music sources (optional)

The complete studio program, designed for schools that are *really* serious about television production, encompasses almost every aspect of audio and video production. A second news reader is added to the set, and the microphones are connected to an audio mixer. The microphone sound is combined by a student operating the audio mixer. The audio mixer may also accommodate the sound from the segment VCR and a cassette player for music openings and endings. A second camcorder may also be used; both camcorders would then be connected to a video switcher, operated by another student. The program can be further enhanced by using a character generator to produce electronic titles (fig. 2.2).

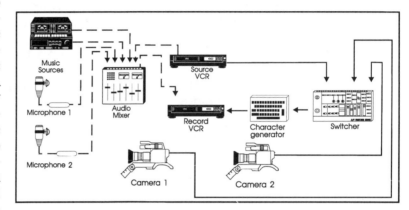

Fig. 2.2. Complete studio show.

Producing a complete studio program is definitely not a task for either beginning television production students or the teacher. This type of program, however, can be developed over several years by adding a new item of equipment or a new technique each year.

The Magazine Format

Some elementary and middle school media specialists and teachers produce a magazine-type program for their school instead of, or in addition to, the programs listed above. The magazine format allows students to work on video segments over a designated time period. Selected students are videotaped introducing these segments to the audience. These intros are then edited together with the segments to produce a weekly or biweekly program for the school.

Formation of a Student News Team

Depending on the type of program you have selected, you need from two or three to nearly a dozen students to help in the program production. Here are some suggestions when deciding which students to include in your program production.

- Ask teachers for suggestions. Teachers can determine which students are interested in working on the team. Make sure that each student recommended can afford to miss a few minutes of class each day.

- Formulate a simple application for the students to complete. Ask for teacher recommendations in the areas of responsibility, reading ability, and punctuality.

- Interview each student to make sure that he or she is willing to create the type of show that the school needs. Some students may only be interested in the "whiz-bang" nature of television, while having very little interest in producing an announcement program.

- Include students from many grade levels. Don't limit your crew to the smartest students in the highest grade level.

- Ask the students about certain jobs that they may like to do. To a first-grader, the task of loading a tape into a VCR and pressing "play" may seem exciting. Some students will like to operate cameras, VCRs, and microphones, but shun appearing on camera.

- Make sure to rotate jobs throughout the school year. Each qualified student should have the opportunity to experiment with talent, audio, and video tasks.

Several job assignments can exist for a news show. These include:

Anchor. Two or three students can be selected to read announcements on a rotating basis.

Camera operator. Among this person's duties would be setting up the camcorder on a tripod, turning the camcorder on, creating the correct shot, and fading out as the show concludes.

Audio technician. On a simple show, this person's duties would include connection and placement of the external microphone. On a more complex show, operation of the audio mixer would be added.

VCR operator. The VCR operator cues, loads, and plays all segments and records the program. Even if the program is shown live, it is nice to record the program so the students involved in production can see the result.

Director. This student would give a simple countdown at the beginning of the program, and tell the VCR operator when to begin segments. The director could also help in organizing the announcements before the show begins.

Segment team. Three or four students could be assigned the task of shooting interesting classroom or school activities. They could also shoot regular program features or special reports.

Avoid creating meaningless jobs, such a set decorator (responsible for changing the bulletin board paper) and lighting technician (responsible for turning on the overhead fluorescent lights). Students quickly become aware of the fact that these roles really aren't essential to the program's production.

Also remember that it is quite natural for some students to become bored with any activity. Expect some of the students to drop out of the program during the year, even though they may be doing a good job. Most schools have enough students interested in television production to maintain a complete crew.

News Show Segment Creation

Adding video segments to your news show provides an excellent opportunity for achieving school content objectives in an entertaining, informative way. Each video segment will probably be about a minute long and consist of three or four different camera angles. Segments can be quite simple, such as showing students singing in music class, or quite complex, such as editing together a series of first-aid tips. Some segments may consist of a single-shot interview with a student or teacher. No matter how intricate or complex the segment production, students and faculty members will enjoy seeing themselves and their friends on your program.

Segment Ideas

If you look around your school, you can probably generate several ideas for regular program features, as well as one-time productions. Here are some ideas that have worked at other elementary and middle schools.

My Favorite Book. Students and teachers hold up their favorite book from the media center and tell why they like it.

Pet of the Week. From hamsters to goldfish to turtles, many elementary school classrooms have pets. Feature a different pet each week, and ask the students how they take care of it.

Meet the Teacher or Meet the Student. To paraphrase Andy Warhol, everybody will be famous for a few minutes. Interviewing a different person each week for no particular reason shows the students that everyone is important at your school.

Focus on Careers. Ask parents to stop by the school and tell about their careers.

Artist of the Week. Ask teachers to provide sample artwork from their classes. Videotape the artwork, or use it to decorate the news set.

Physical Education Activities. Videotape students during P.E. and interview the coach about the importance of physical activity and exercise.

Teacher of the Month/Student of the Month. Most schools have these award programs anyway. Make sure to feature the winners on your program.

Focus on School Workers. Ask the noninstructional employees about their jobs on camera. Focus on the job requirements and responsibilities.

Nutrition Corner. Go beyond the standard lunch menu to ask the school cafeteria manager about the importance of each item on the menu.

Health Report. Ask the school nurse to provide information about safety and first aid.

Special events can also be covered with video segments. Here are some ideas.

• Math, science, and book fairs

• PTA/PTSA activities

• Special holiday events

• Theme shows, for example, "Black History Week"

Video Segment Shot Selection

Before your students go out to create these segments, talk to them about the four basic shots used in segment creation.

1. *The establishing shot.* This shot shows the viewer exactly where the action is taking place (fig. 2.3).

This could be a classroom, the media center, or the playground.

Fig. 2.3. Establishing shot.

2. *The interview shot.* For simple interviews, use a two-shot waist shot. This shot is created by having both the interviewer and the subject in the shot, and including the area from the waist up (fig. 2.4.).

3. *The close-up.* Sometimes the segment works best when the interviewer is not on camera. This works best when the subject (person you are interviewing) is shot as a close-up (fig. 2.5 on page 66). Make sure that students know the importance of getting close-ups of other items as well. Teach

Fig. 2.4. Interview shot.

the students to "fill the screen" with the subject.

4. *Over-the-shoulder shot.* When the focus of the shot is on students working, try an over-the-shoulder-shot. The over-the-shoulder shot is like a close-up and includes the shoulder and part of the head of the person performing the task (fig. 2.6). In effect, the camera is peeking over the person's shoulder. This shot brings the viewer into the action and adds perspective to the shot.

Fig. 2.5. Close-up.

Fig. 2.6. Over-the-shoulder shot.

Teach these four basic shots *before* the students go out to shoot segments. Make brief shooting assignments to ensure that students can create these shots without cutting off someone's head or swaying too much. For example, tell one of your television production students to walk around school and shoot four over-the-shoulder shots. When the student returns, critique the tape with the student and plan more practice sessions.

Emphasize planning *before* the shoot. Use the storyboard form in figure 2.7.

Editing the Segments

The process of deck-to-deck editing is fully explained in chapter 5, beginning on page 94. Although you may need to edit a few of your segments, most of the simpler ones will probably be fine as shot.

Announcement Forms

Sample announcement forms are included at the end of this chapter (see fig. 2.8 on page 68). Provide one or two places around school for teachers to pick up blank forms, and set a deadline for return of them.

A successful school announcement show can be a rewarding, educational experience for the student team, the media specialist, and the audience. The task of the faculty member is to assemble the proper equipment, select the student team, and provide ideas and opportunities for segment creation and student involvement.

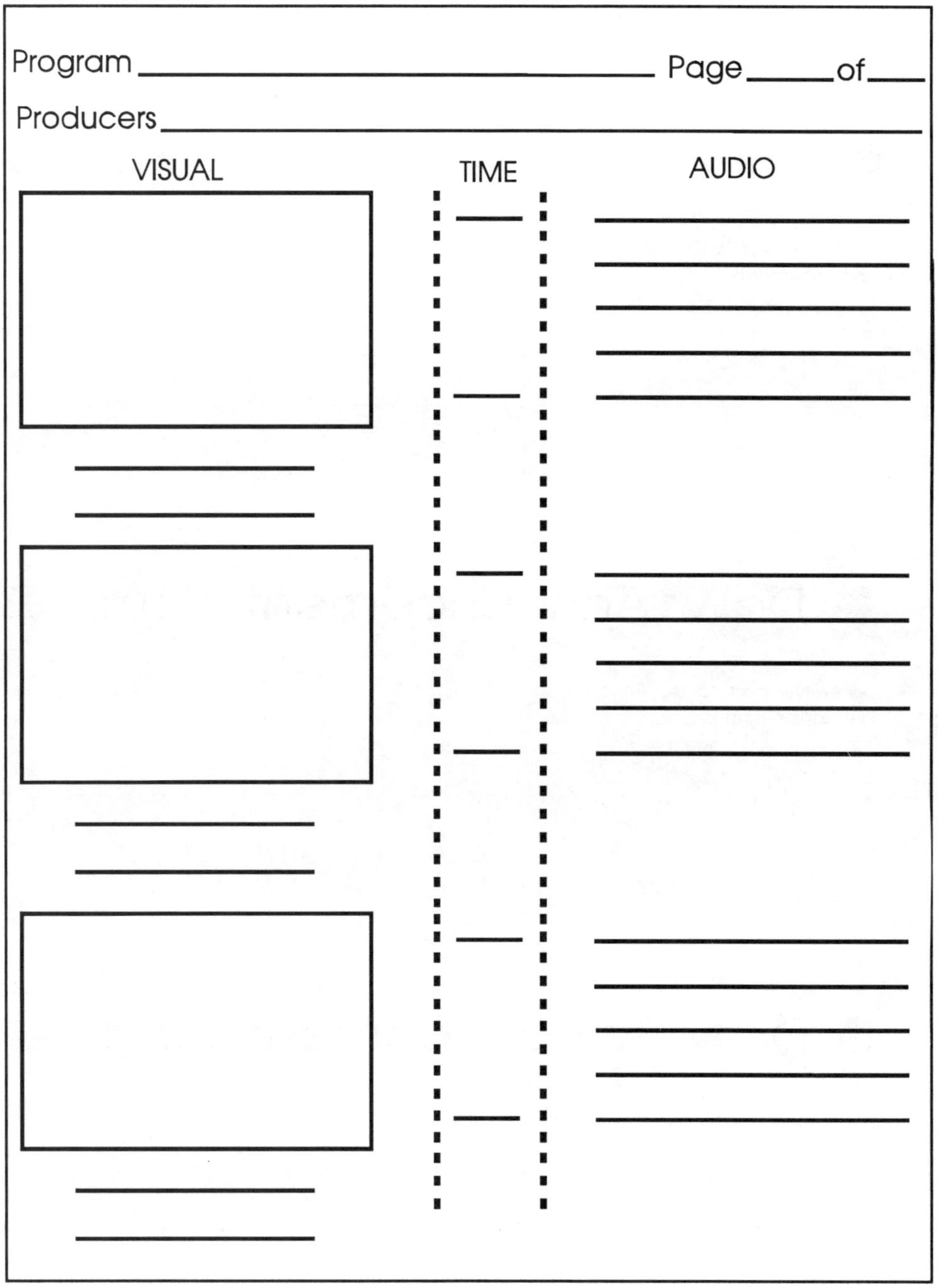

VISUAL	TIME	AUDIO

Program _____ Page _____ of _____

Producers _____

Fig. 2.7. Storyboard.

Diligent, consistent work in this area allows the school announcement program to transcend the standard "pledge of allegiance and lunch menu" format, creating an entertaining, informative, essential part of the school day.

♟ Daily Announcement Form 🎬

Return To:_____

Dates Needed To Be Announced:_____

Announcement:_____

_____

_____

_____

_____

_____

_____

_____

Teacher Signature:_____

♟ Daily Announcement Form 🎬

Return To:_____

Dates Needed To Be Announced:_____

Announcement:_____

_____

_____

_____

_____

_____

_____

_____

Teacher Signature:_____

♟ Daily Announcement Form 🎬

Return To:_____

Dates Needed To Be Announced:_____

Announcement:_____

_____

_____

_____

_____

_____

_____

_____

Teacher Signature:_____

Fig. 2.8. Blank announcement forms.

3 VIDEOTAPE SERVICES FOR YOUR SCHOOL

Media specialists and teachers frequently have the opportunity to provide videotaping services for their school. Because the media specialist is the caretaker of the camcorder and other assorted audiovisual goodies, the faculty and administration often contact the media center to request that a guest speaker, a classroom activity, or an assembly program be videotaped (fig. 3.1 on page 70).

There are many reasons for providing these services. The most obvious is the unique nature of the experience. If an expert on conservation speaks to your school and brings along an endangered animal indigenous to your area, the videotape of such a presentation could be quite valuable. The tape could then be played each year when students study endangered species. Students will enjoy and appreciate a videotape program created at their school especially for them. A resourceful media specialist could accrue a small library of these programs over the school year. Another advantage of recording guest speakers and class experiences is that you can acquire videotapes of a local nature. A videotape about the history of your city, for example, may not be available anywhere else. Local pioneers often visit schools to tell the children about life in their city before cars, busses, and air conditioning. Finally, most media specialists will find videotaping to be a rewarding experience. The knowledge that students for years to come will view a videotape program that you have produced touches the same emotions that encourage most media specialists to create excellent media centers.

Of course, video programs worth keeping don't just happen. They are the result of knowledge and experience in video production. In the next few pages, we'll explain some basic approaches to providing videotape services to your school, including classroom recordings and assembly programs.

Videotaping a Class Session

There's a lot of excitement in an elementary or middle school classroom. Teachers frequently host guest speakers from the community, conduct simple science experiments, and dramatize exciting stories, all for the benefit of their students. Almost every teacher can point to a day that he or she would like to see and present again through the use of videotape. Faculty members can help fill that need by providing video production services.

Fig. 3.1. Videotaping request form.

Request For Videotaping Services

Requester _____ Today's Date _____

Type of Service: _____ Guest Speaker
                         _____ Class Activity
                         _____ Assembly Program
                         _____ Other

Date Requested _____   Time _____ AM PM
Duration (Time) of Activity _____   Location/Room # _____
Description of Activity _____

_____

_____

_____

_____

If guest speaker, name and telephone number _____

_____

Projected use for tape _____

_____

_____

PLEASE RETURN THIS FORM TO THE MEDIA CENTER AT LEAST ONE WEEK
BEFORE THE DATE REQUESTED. THANK YOU.

PLEASE DO NOT WRITE BELOW THIS LINE

_____

_____

PRODUCTION NOTES:

Videotaping a Guest Speaker/Instructor-Centered Class Session

Many videotaping opportunities will involve a guest speaker or a teacher presenting a program to the class. Videotaping this session usually involves getting a nice shot of the front of the room.

Equipment

You will need a basic setup for videotaping such a class session. A simple *camcorder* can record the footage. The *videotape* that you use should be of high quality so that the program can be played many times without the loss of picture quality. Because the class session will last more than a few minutes, use a *tripod* to provide a steady, tireless shot. If an electrical outlet is readily available, plan on using the camcorder's *AC power supply*. Using power from a wall socket will save worry over battery power and eliminate the possibility that the camcorder will run out of battery power during the presentation.

Because what the speaker says will be at least as important as what the speaker does, sound quality is vital to this project. Don't rely on the camcorder's built-in microphone. Instead, opt for one of the following:

- *A shotgun microphone* can be mounted on the camcorder. Its extreme unidirectional pick up pattern will capture the sound of the guest speaker or teacher from across the room while excluding extraneous noise.

- *A lavaliere microphone* will work if you have a nice, long length of microphone cable. The guest could simply clip this microphone to his or her clothing and forget about it. Of course, you would need to educate the speaker about the cable length so that the microphone is not jerked out of the camcorder when the speaker takes an extra step. Also, the lavaliere microphone would not pick up any questions from the audience, and would be ineffective in picking up audience reaction or applause.

- *A wireless microphone* especially a wireless lavaliere, offers an intriguing alternative. The problem of microphone cable is eliminated. However, the lack of audience pick up is still a disadvantage. The shotgun microphone mounted on the camcorder seems to be the winner here.

- Don't forget to use a set of *headphones* with an external microphone. Otherwise, a break in the microphone cable or a malfunction in the microphone itself will go undetected until the disappointed videographer returns to the media center to view the tape. Because camcorders often do not provide an amplified audio signal, the videographer is never quite sure if the microphone is working or not. By gently scratching the surface of the microphone before taping begins, the videographer should be able to hear the unique scratching sound clearly through the headphones. If he or she doesn't hear a signal, a check of the headphones is in order. If they are broken, no microphone in the world will make a sound for you!

An external *video monitor* or *television* may be used for presentations that last more than a few minutes. Connect the television/monitor to the camcorder's output, and you can see the picture that you are recording without continually squinting into the viewfinder. The checklist in figure 3.2, on page 73, should help you organize your equipment for each session.

Technique

Here are some tips when videotaping a speaker/instructor-centered class session.

- Make sure that the speaker knows about and endorses the videotaping ahead of time. The arrival of the media specialist and camcorder should be a welcomed blessing, not an unpleasant surprise.

- Arrange and test your equipment before you leave the media center. Try to avoid situations that will require you to run back to the equipment room for a forgotten item. If possible, bring an extra microphone, headphone set, and even a couple of batteries for "Plan B."

- Plan to arrive early. Ask the speaker to briefly go over the program with you. Tell the speaker exactly what you're doing and why. Some people who are great with an audience get very nervous when the camera rolls. Consider placing a small piece of masking tape over your camcorder's tally light; something about that little red light makes people very uncomfortable. Ask about any "surprises" in the program so that you'll be ready. Determine the action radius of the program.

- Will any small items be presented? If possible, place your camera so that you can zoom in for a close-up. Ask the speaker for the opportunity to videotape those items (e.g., rocks, small animals).

- Will a question-and-answer session be included in the program? If so, position your camera so that you can easily swing around to get a shot of the questioner. This position may be on the side of the room. If no question-and-answer session is planned, the best spot for the camera is probably in the center of the room, about halfway back.

- Beware of backlighting that will affect your auto iris (see "Camcorder Controls and Adjustments—Iris Controls" in chapter 1). This lighting may include open windows or blinds, overhead projectors, and incandescent lighting. Move your camera to avoid these problems.

- Make sure to roll tape a minute or two before the program begins. Teachers using the tape in the future can cue the tape before they show it. This minor inconvenience is preferable to the possibility of missing the first few seconds of the presentation.

- If handouts or overhead transparencies (which don't videotape very well) are part of the presentation, make sure to obtain an extra set. Laminate the handouts and store them with the videotape. Make a photocopy of the overheads and store them as well (with the speaker's permission, of course).

Fig. 3.2. Equipment checklist.

Equipment Checklist

Project _____ Room # _____

Date _____ Time _____ Contact _____

_____

_____

	Needed	Taken	Returned
camcorder			
tripod			
batteries (# ____)			
AC adapter			
multi-outlet power strip			
electrical extension cord			
monitor/television			
cable (RF/BNC/phono)			
media cart			
hand-held microphone			
shotgun microphone			
lavaliere microphone			
wireless microphone system			
microphone stand			
microphone cable			
impedance adapter			
_____			
_____			
_____			
_____			
_____			

Production Notes:

- Make sure to thank the guest speaker for the opportunity to videotape the presentation. If no copyrighted material was used, offer to duplicate the tape for the speaker's personal use.

The camcorder can certainly be a valuable tool for producing instructional materials. Plan to tape programs as they arise. Train a small group of interested students to help with the task; they may be able to eventually perform duties unsupervised. The addition of the guest speaker or teacher's presentation will make a valuable, inexpensive contribution to your media center collection.

Videotaping Student/Group-Centered Activities

Many of the worthwhile activities in your school's classrooms take place while students are working in small groups or using learning centers to explore new areas of study. These activities are certainly worth videotaping so that others can see what a teacher is doing in the classroom. Maybe such a videotape could be presented at each faculty meeting. "The Idea Video" could become a valuable, entertaining part of each meeting!

The equipment and techniques for shooting student-centered activities are very similar to those used for shooting guest speakers, with a few notable exceptions.

- Arrive early and talk with the teacher about all of the activities in the classroom. Plan the different areas that you will need to shoot.

- Make sure to shoot most of your footage from the low, student angle. Don't make the "towering teacher" video that looks down on the tops of the students' heads from above. Kneel down, or sit in a student chair.

- Arrange to have an assistant who will conduct brief interviews for you. Ask the students and teacher about the project (e.g., what they like, what they learn). You may even want to add a brief, on-camera introduction to give the segment an even more professional appearance.

- Although the raw footage that you shoot will be quite entertaining, consider performing some simple deck-to-deck editing, as will be explained in chapter 5.

- Because you will be shooting most shots "on the shoulder," you will probably need to abandon the AC adapter in favor of battery power for your camcorder. Make sure to take an extra battery.

- Consider the composition that will make your video interesting. You will definitely want to include a lot of close-ups. The over-the-shoulder shot, in which the videographer shoots from behind the student at a 45-degree angle, would be quite effective in this situation. The over-the-shoulder shot gets the audience involved in the project and helps to maintain proper size perspective.

- Recognize that these segments will likely be much shorter than your guest-speaker tapes. A single classroom activity tape will last about 10 minutes.

- Make sure that each segment can stand alone without any extra explanation to the viewer. This will enable other teachers to watch the segment in the future and facilitate the training of new teachers in your school.

The creation of a small library of classroom activity tapes will make a valuable addition to your A/V collection. Your colleagues, who tend to be somewhat isolated from other professionals during the day, will be able to see all of the exciting activities in the classrooms. When presented at faculty meetings and in-services, these taped segments will stimulate discussion and creativity in your school.

Videotaping School Assembly Programs

Most schools hold a variety of assembly, awards, dramatic, and musical programs throughout the year. Although the kindergarten program may be no more than a few simple rhymes and songs, the middle school program can be quite long and complex. Here are some tips for videotaping these programs.

- Place the camera about halfway back in the auditorium to obtain a good shot. If the seats are not gradually elevated (like a movie theatre), arrange to have the seats in front of you free or occupied by short people. You don't want the back of someone's head in the middle of all of your shots.

- Plan to use your camcorder's AC adapter, not a battery. If the battery completely discharges during the program, you will lose power and, of course, have to stop taping until you load a new battery. Using the AC adapter guarantees an uninterrupted power supply.

- Always use a tripod.

- Don't forget to white-balance the camera. If the program uses special stage lighting, the white balancing should be done with those lights on.

- Establish your shot, white-balance your camera, and then put the camera on standby. Doing so saves power, camera wear, and maintains the white balance. A camera on standby takes about two seconds to power up; the camera that is "off" takes about 10 seconds. That difference in time could make you miss the beginning of the assembly program.

- Plan for audio as well as video. Consider using a shotgun microphone. If the program consists of a single guest speaker, investigate the use of a wireless microphone (perhaps lavaliere) for the speaker.

- Beware of using too many pans and zooms. Unless the focus of action moves a lot on the stage, you will need to use very few shots. During a school play, zooming in on one part of the action may cause you to miss another part. If you are videotaping a single speaker, you may want to alternate among a long shot (full body), a medium shot (knees up), and a bust shot (chest up) of the speaker. Hold each shot for at least a few minutes. Too many pans or zooms can distract from the videotaped program.

- Become aware of copyright law as it relates to making copies of your tape. Generally speaking, you can make a tape for the purpose of allowing the director and participants to critique their performances only. Presentations of copyrighted dramatic works cannot be duplicated without paying royalties to the publishers. For example, if your school's drama club produced the play *The Hobbit*, you would not be able to make a copy of the tape for each cast member; however, the original could be shown to the class/cast for review. A guest speaker presenting an original program may allow copies to be made for neighboring elementary or middle schools. For example: A police officer comes to your school to speak on the dangers of alcohol and drug use. The officer would probably agree to duplication of the program for the other elementary schools in your district. In any case, always ask your district media center before duplicating *any* videotape.

Whether the subject is a classroom speaker, a creative student activity, or an assembly program, you, the media specialist, will probably have the opportunity to provide videotaping services for your school. Awareness of video production equipment and strategies can make this activity another important link in the education process.

4 USING VIDEO TO TEACH MEDIA SKILLS

Most school media centers have a curriculum for teaching students how to use the library media center. Kindergartners are taught the location and purpose of the school library media center, proper checkout procedures, and selection of easy materials. Older primary students work with the card catalog, audiovisual materials, and research strategies. Middle school students learn search skills with electronic resources. Whether formal, consisting of presentations and worksheets, or casual, consisting of talking with the students one on one, the media center curriculum is certainly an important part of the elementary and middle school experience.

Probably one of the most useful tasks that a district-level media specialist can perform is to organize and standardize the teaching of library media skills throughout the school district. In fact, many states require districts to formulate such a plan. By stating these objectives in behavioral terms, media specialists throughout the district can teach important skills, and a child who moves across town will be able to begin to use the media center immediately upon arrival.

Several Orange County, Florida, media specialists gathered to formulate such a plan. In the next few pages, we'll select an objective from each grade level of the plan and propose the use of video to teach that skill. Because each library media center is different, we have resisted the urge to designate the specific book titles and authors. But by adapting these plans in your center, you can provide a creative, memorable exercise in traditional media and video production.

Activity:	**Video Story-Telling**
Grade Level:	kindergarten
Objective:	To encourage kindergarten students to participate in story-telling activities.
Equipment:	camcorder, tripod, power supply, microphone, videotape
Instructions:	Assemble groups of 10-12 students. Present to each group a premise for a story (a little puppy travels to the city, a little bird sits in a nest, etc.) and have the group create the story as each student tells the next event of the story on-camera. Then, play back the videotape and ask students to retell the story; if they wish, they can create alternate endings to the story. Make sure to play a representation of the stories for the entire group.

Activity:	**My Favorite Book**
Grade Level:	grade 1
Objective:	To identify the main idea of a story.
Equipment:	camcorder, tripod, power supply, microphone, videotape
Instructions:	Have the students find their favorite book in the media center. (It's OK if several students select the same book.) Ask them to look through the book and perhaps retell the story to a media specialist or clerk. Then ask the students about the story and why they like it. Ask them to tell the story in one sentence.

Once the students are comfortable with this activity, ask them to hold their favorite book while you videotape them telling the main idea of the story and why they like it. Show the results to the class and feature a "My Favorite Book" on your daily news show.

Activity:	**Our Video Storybook**
Grade Level:	grade 2
Objective:	To develop story sequencing activities.
Equipment:	camcorder, tripod, power supply, microphone, videotape, crayons and markers, art paper, masking tape
Instructions:	Provide a quality picture book for each group of six or seven students. The media specialist, teacher, and clerk should supervise the oral reading of the books and ask questions about the plot to make sure that all of the students understand the story. Then assign a part of the story for each student to illustrate. At this point, you may need to read the story again.

Once the students have completed their drawings, attach the drawings to the wall or a bulletin board. Videotape the first drawing by placing the camcorder close to the picture. (You may need to use the macro lens if the picture is quite small.) As the picture is videotaped, have the student read his or her part of the story into the microphone. Press the "pause" button on the camcorder between photos. Don't worry about mistakes. Simply recue the tape and rerecord the student's presentation. The result is a video storybook that the entire class can enjoy.

Remove the drawings after videotaping is complete and make them available to the audience. While viewing the story, the audience can arrange the actual drawings in the order that they appear on the screen.

Activity:	**Exploring Nonfiction Books**
Grade Level:	grade 3
Objective:	To identify major classes in the Dewey Decimal system and familiarize students with materials found in that area.

Equipment: camcorder, tripod, power supply, microphone, videotape, decorated shoe box with slips of paper

Instructions: Introduce the concept of the Dewey Decimal system to the students. Then have each student draw from the shoe box a slip of paper on which is written a Dewey call number that students would find interesting. Each student must then use the call number to find a book on the shelf, examine its content, then report to the video area. There, he or she is interviewed by the media specialist on videotape about the topic of the book. For added fun, the media specialist could wear a trenchcoat and hat, and conduct "person-on-the-street" interviews about the books, or dress as a police officer investigating the Dewey Decimal system. The end result is a videotape that informs and entertains.

Activity: **Author Profile**

Grade Level: grade 4

Objective: To define and locate author cards in the card catalog and learn more about authors.

Equipment: camcorder, tripod, power supply, microphone, videotape, crayons and markers, art paper

Instructions: Each student or small group of students should select a favorite author. (The media specialist should provide a list of authors with multiple titles in the media center.) The student or group could prepare a brief biography of the author and use the card catalog to locate and list the books by the author available in the media center. They can then make graphics using crayons, markers, and art paper, and videotape the graphics. Students can narrate biographical events while showing a photo or drawing of the author. Then, students could appear on camera telling about their favorite book by the author. The final result would be a two-minute video program about the life and work of the author.

Activity: **Our Community History**

Grade Level: grade 5 and up

Objective: To use community resources for recreational and informational purposes.

Equipment: camcorder, tripod, power supply, microphone, videotape, title card supplies (markers, paper, etc.)

Instructions: By coordinating with the classroom teachers, the media specialist can undertake the project of creating historical programs about the community. Local historical societies and PTA members can help identify local pioneers. These individuals could be invited to your school to be interviewed about what life was like in your community years ago. Encourage the invited guests to bring photo albums and videotape the pictures using your macro lens. Students can use reference books to help fill in the gaps about your community's history. This is obviously an involved project, but the students who work on it will learn valuable lessons about using resources outside the media center to complete reports and projects. The finished project, whether edited with graphics, or simply shot with the camcorder, will be a valuable resource for your school and community.

Activity:	**Video Scavenger Hunt**
Grade Level:	grade 6 and up
Objective:	To identify and locate a wide variety of media center materials, using the card catalog and their media center experience.
Equipment:	camcorder, power supply, videotape
Instructions:	Divide the group into teams of four or five students, and provide each team with a camcorder and a videotape. Each team is then given a list of media center items that they must videotape to complete the scavenger hunt. Formulate the list to achieve specific objectives, such as "Find a magazine article about the space shuttle" (using *Reader's Guide* and periodicals), "Find a collection of mystery stories" (card catalog and story collections), "Find a book about snakes" (card catalog and Dewey Decimal collection). Don't forget to include questions specific to your library media center.

As the students locate the items requested, have them stand on-camera holding the resource and explaining how they found it. Make sure all groups finish within the allotted time. Be ready to provide "hints" to avoid frustrating negative experiences. Show all tapes to the class, and make sure that the students know *how* they found their items.

Obviously, this activity should be adapted to the specific strengths and objectives of your center. For example, you may include computer or A/V items in your "hunt." Whatever items the list contains, the use of the camcorder will add excitement to this replacement for the pencil-and-paper "fact search."

Our suggestions for teaching media skills are not all-inclusive; they are meant to get your creative juices flowing. The sky's the limit when it comes to using video to teach the media curriculum of your library media center.

Source:	*Library Media Skills K-12* (document F7ELIB148), Orange County Public Schools, Orlando, Florida, 1991.

5 PRODUCING VIDEOTAPE PROGRAMS FOR YOUR SCHOOL

Many schools have produced videotape programs of their schools. This may seem like an impossible task to media specialists and teachers inexperienced in video production. So, in this chapter, we'll explain the procedure of producing such a program and walk through the production of a simple school orientation tape.

There are many reasons for producing short videotape programs at the school level. Probably the most profound reason for creating such a program is the unique product that results. Most schools would love to have a videotape program, for example, about the specific opportunities and policies of the school. Another reason for producing videotape programs is the ability of the medium of television to relate information. Parents and students are much more likely to watch an interesting video than read a lengthy handbook or report. A third reason is the ability to make identical presentations using the video program. Popping in a tape relieves the stress of needing the same presenter at every meeting, and time and distance constraints are eliminated. A tape could be available for checkout by parents for viewing at home, as well as shown at school orientations and PTA meetings. Clearly, videotape production is a worthwhile activity for the school media program.

Throughout this chapter, we'll use an example to guide us through the production process. Our video project will be about Polk Avenue Elementary School, which would like to have a videotape introducing students, parents, and community members to the school, its policies, and programs of instruction. We'll be using terms and equipment discussed in chapter 1, so now might be a good time to quickly review that section.

Here are some terms that apply to the production of video programs that we really haven't talked about yet.

Preproduction. The activities in a video production that take place before the raw footage is shot. These activities include brainstorming, scripting, storyboarding, and planning.

Production. Recording the raw audio and video used in the video program. This includes shooting in a studio, making videotape in the field, and gathering music and sound effects.

> **Postproduction.** Making a completed video program out of the production footage and sound, including evaluating the raw footage, adding graphics, editing, and audio dubbing.

Preproduction Activities

As stated above, the preproduction activities take place before the raw footage is shot. In many respects, the preproduction is the most important part of the videotaping process. Without preproduction, a media specialist may as well just begin shooting raw footage with no rhyme or reason. The result? The frustration of wading through hours of videotape looking for one shot that you probably don't have. Preproduction can save hours *and* headaches. There are four important preproduction activities: (1) brainstorming, (2) scripting, (3) storyboarding, and (4) planning.

Brainstorming

The first important step in any creative production is brainstorming. As most media specialists and classroom teachers know, brainstorming is an exercise in which ideas are mentioned quickly and written down without any discussion. As the group listens to each idea, creative group members begin to merge the best parts of the ideas together to come up with the best approach or solution. Brainstorming also works well when trying to determine the approach for your video project.

But before the brainstorming process can be productive, you need to resolve certain issues about your project to ensure that it will be useful as well as creative. Following are some of these issues.

Audience

Determine the audience for your program. Will your program be viewed by parents, students, administrators, or all audiences? A good video program speaks to its audience. For our example, the Polk Avenue Elementary School program will be aimed at elementary students, parents, and community members.

Objectives

What are the objectives of your program? In other words, after watching your program, what should the viewer know, or be able to do? A program that has a general, "feel good" objective is very different from a program that intends to teach a task or inform a group about a policy or procedure.

These objectives don't have to be stated in the educational/behavioral mode; after all, it's difficult to have quantifiable goals for a public relations or orientation video. Just force yourself to verbalize your intended outcome. For example, our objectives for the Polk Avenue Elementary video are:

1. To introduce the school to new students, parents, and community members.

2. To help form positive attitudes about the school.

3. To inform the audience about the history of the school.

Funding

Determine your costs for production of this project and exactly how you're going to meet these costs. (See figure 5.1 on page 84.) Don't panic— school orientation programs are not Hollywood big budget productions. Still, there are some costs that have to be covered.

In our example, the Polk Avenue program will incur the following costs:

blank tape for recording raw footage - $15

professional-quality tape for editing master - $7

raw materials for handmade graphics - $10

videotape for making five copies - $15

Total: $47

Fortunately, because the principal knows a bargain when she sees one, she's agreed to foot the bill and provide release time and gas money for trips to the district office for postproduction, if needed.

Time

Determine the length of your video. Try to make the program as concise as possible to avoid audience boredom. As the old expression goes, it's best to leave 'em wanting just a little bit more. Overly long, exhaustive programs can bury your objectives.

In our example program, after examining our objectives, we decide to shoot for the seven-minute mark. This may surprise those readers who have produced 15- or 20-minute programs in the past. Remember, the video should not replace the welcome by the principal, the student/parent handbook, or the school open house. Instead, the video program should be used to *augment* the orientation process and enrich parent and student perception of the school.

Approach and Attitude

At this point, it is important to establish the proper approach and attitude that you wish this project to have. Video programs tend to take on an identity of their own—an identity created by you, the producer. Decide if your program should be humorous and lighthearted, or serious and somber.

Currently, the dominant style of video production is to make the program just a little bit less formal than one would expect. (At a recent corporate video contest, the winner was a seafood restaurant chain that had created an instructional video to educate local chefs about the preparation of a new lobster dinner. What was

Fig. 5.1. Funding worksheet.

Funding Worksheet for _____

<u>Blank Tape</u>
   Videotape

	Length	Quantity	Unit Price	Total
T -	_____	_____	_____	$ _____
T -	_____	_____	_____	_____
T -	_____	_____	_____	_____
T -	_____	_____	_____	_____

   Audiotape
      C - _____   _____   _____ $ _____

<u>Equipment</u>
   Equipment purchases _____ $ _____
   Equipment rental _____ _____
   A/V services (editing, etc.) _____ _____

<u>Music</u>
   Buy-out _____ $ _____
   Lease/performance fees _____ _____

<u>Materials</u>
   Graphics creation _____ $ _____
   Costumes/props _____ _____
   Office supplies _____ _____
   Other _____ _____

<u>Transportation</u>
   Gasoline _____ $ _____
   Tolls, other _____ _____

<u>Videotape Duplication</u> (if copyright-cleared)
   Number of copies _____ x Unit price $ ____ $ _____

                    Total Funding Required $ _____

surprising about this winning selection was that it was "rapped" with a hip-hop music background by a talented woman of considerable size dressed in a lobster suit, dancing in front of a sea-blue background.) Don't be afraid to make your audience smile. An audience having fun is an audience paying attention.

For our elementary video program, we have decided to take a moderately lighthearted approach.

Resources

Make a list of any special resources that you have available that can be useful in your video production. Ask around. You may be surprised at the resources available in your school. A friend of a teacher's uncle may be able to give you an airplane ride over the school to obtain some great aerial footage. Some veteran teachers may have photographs of the school from earlier decades. How did your school look in the '50s? The principal may have the school's blueprints tucked away in a filing cabinet. Could a friend arrange for a hot air balloon to fly over the school at daybreak for an exciting opening? The possibilities for making your program exceptional are endless.

In our example: Polk Avenue Elementary School was one of the first elementary schools built in the area. It was constructed in the 1920s. Since then the city has changed dramatically. Fortunately, the school has a small archive of photographs and drawings depicting the school's history. One of the school's teachers is also a history buff who recently created 1920s-era clothing for a play in his class. Another teacher has offered a few reels of super 8mm home movies that she took when her class performed a play in the 1970s.

Strengths and Weaknesses

At this point, determine the strong points and weak points of all of the preproduction information you've amassed. What aspects could be improved? What aspects should be emphasized?

In our example, the strengths include the rich history of the school and the photographic documentation, the costumes from the era, and the funding from our principal. The weaknesses are the somewhat general objectives and the large age difference in our audience members. The strengths are quite strong, and will probably help form the program, while our weaknesses are unavoidable, considering the scope of the project.

Scripting

Now that we have a good idea of the direction our project will take, it's time to turn on the word processor (or at least sharpen our pencils) and begin to formulate the script.

Before you begin actually writing the words that will lead the viewer through the program, prepare a one- to two- page treatment of the program. On the top of the page, write the working title of the program. Underneath, copy the objectives that you created earlier. On the next few lines, script or describe the opening minute of your project. Then proceed to outline the project, just as you would outline an essay or a speech. Make sure to note interviews that you plan to conduct with the principal (she *is* paying for this!), students, parents, etc. After your outline is completed, write a few sentences about how the project will end.

This treatment should serve as your compass throughout your production and postproduction. Don't discard it when shooting begins. Continue to review and revise the treatment as needed so that your program will maintain its singular focus and achieve its objectives.

After your treatment is complete, you are ready to write the first draft of your script. This, no doubt, sounds like a major task, but realistically, the script for a seven-minute program will probably be only three or four typed, double-spaced pages. Here are some tips that should guide you in your scriptwriting process.

- Remember your audience and write to their vocabulary level. If your audience has a wide range of levels, write for the lowest level, keeping the highest level in mind as well.

- Beware of wordiness and pedantry. Write for the typical person, not the superintendent with a doctorate in education. Instead of "Here at Polk Avenue, we strive to fulfill the diverse cognitive and affective needs of our students," write "Here at Polk Avenue we not only teach the children, we care about them, too."

- Keep it simple. Make your project enjoyable instead of tiresome.

- Show, don't tell. Many poor scripts are filled with "This is the cafeteria. . .", "This is the media center. . .", "This is the first-grade class. . .", and so on. Write interesting, complete sentences. Instead of "This is our cafeteria. Most students eat in the cafeteria. The cafeteria lunch is a well-balanced meal," write "Our cafeteria serves about 500 meals a day. That's almost 100,000 meals a year. The students like hamburgers and hot dogs best of all, but the cafeteria staff makes sure that students are also served milk, fruits, and vegetables." Keep the script light and conversational. Unless you are showing something quite out of the ordinary ("This is Waldo the hippopotamus, the pet in Ms. Bishop's room."), you probably don't need to tell the audience what it is they're looking at.

- Don't play politics. Spend a few minutes/hours talking with administration, faculty, and staff about the parts of the school that should be emphasized in your school orientation tape. Talk about the school, not just your favorite parts.

- Continuously review and revise your script. As new opportunities arise, change your script to accommodate their inclusion. Remember, your script is a "living document." Let it change and grow—but don't let it grow *too big*!

Storyboarding

After you have completed your script, you should storyboard your project. Storyboarding is that part of the planning process that includes drawing a simple sketch of the desired shot, planning the accompanying audio, and estimating the duration of each element in the program. Simply stated, you need to draw the project before you begin shooting. (See figs. 5.2 and 5.3) Storyboarding may sound difficult, but if you follow these recommendations, it can be quite simple.

Fig. 5.2. Storyboard form.

Program _____ Page _____ of ___

Producers _____

VISUAL	TIME	AUDIO

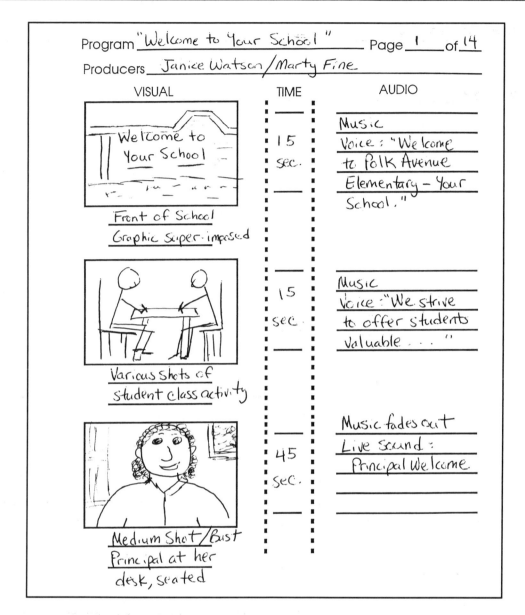

Program "Welcome to Your School"   Page 1 of 14
Producers Janice Watson/Marty Fine

VISUAL	TIME	AUDIO
Front of School Graphic Super-imposed	15 sec.	Music Voice: "Welcome to Polk Avenue Elementary — Your School."
Various shots of student class activity	15 sec.	Music Voice: "We strive to offer students valuable . . ."
Medium Shot/Bust Principal at her desk, seated	45 sec.	Music fades out Live Sound: Principal Welcome

Fig. 5.3. Completed storyboard.

1. Keep it simple. Even if you are an accomplished artist, stick to simple drawings. Remember, storyboards simply serve to remind you of the composition of the shots. Minor details aren't important.

2. Draw the actual shot. Beginning storyboarders often leave too much headroom in the storyboards. Imagine watching your program on a television, and draw the shot you wish to create. If you want a close-up, draw a close-up. Sometimes it helps to close your eyes and visualize the shot before you begin to draw.

3. Consider creative camera angles and points of view. Change the level (height) of your videography occasionally. Perhaps you could make a few shots from the first-grader's point of view.

4. Use the margins for notes. Descriptions can compensate and augment the work of beginning storyboard artists.

5. Use arrows to indicate panning and camera movement.

6. Make a rough estimate of the length of the shot and list that time on the storyboard. If you are editing, plan to roll your tape at least five seconds before the action starts. If you are not editing, remember that most camcorders have a one- or two-second startup time before the image begins recording on the tape. If your principal begins to speak as soon as you push the trigger, you will miss the first few seconds of her comment.

7. Don't forget to storyboard the audio. List the first few words of your script for each shot. Also indicate whether the sound will be "live" (e.g., comments and interviews) or music audio-dubbed in the postproduction phase of the project. Also try to describe the type of music you would like to use.

Before you begin to storyboard, you will need to determine the type of graphics you will use (electronic or hand-drawn) and the editing capabilities you have at your disposal. For example, if you plan to start your project with the title of the school superimposed over a shot of the front of the school, then you need to make sure that you will have a character generator available. If you don't have access to a character generator, you need to determine a creative way to accomplish this task with the hand-drawn techniques described earlier in this book. Also determine your editing capabilities. At the very least, you should be able to perform some basic cuts during deck-to-deck editing. However, if you have access to an elaborate editing system, you may be able to perform video inserts. For example, as your principal talks about the new computer lab in the media center, you will probably be shooting a close-up of the principal. If you can video insert, you can place a shot of the computer lab over the narration. Your knowledge of graphics techniques and editing capabilities needs to be determined before storyboarding begins, as it will greatly affect the planning of your video project.

Experience tells us that storyboarding is a task best performed by individuals, not groups. Undoubtedly, there will be many shots in your project. A discussion about each shot is probably not a wise use of time.

Make copies of the blank storyboard sheet provided in this book (fig. 5.2). (Trust us . . . it's OK. If we say you can do it, you can't go to jail. But you owe us, big-time.) Place the completed storyboard sheets in plastic page holders and put the holders in a three-ring binder. When it's time to shoot, grab the camcorder, the binder, and go!

Planning the Shoot

Make a shooting schedule and make personal contact with each person you wish to interview. Most teachers will need to know a day or two in advance if you're going to videotape their classroom and/or ask them a few questions. Will you be editing this project? If so, it's OK to shoot out of order. Shoot the scenes as they become available. When you edit, you can put them back in the right order.

Make a list of all of the equipment you will need for each shot. This may seem like a simplistic thing to do, but it will be worthwhile if it saves a long walk from the P.E. area to the equipment room for the microphone you forgot. And what's the most-often forgotten item? The blank videotape!

Don't be afraid to make a Plan B. Just try to make Plan B as good as Plan A!

As you can see, the preproduction activities are quite involved and *very* important. Can you imagine making our seven-minute documentary without storyboarding, brainstorming, or scripting? Following the preproduction steps discussed here can make completing this project a painless and rewarding experience.

Production Activities

After all of that preproduction work, it may seem like the rest of the project is "downhill all the way." In a way, that's true. A carefully planned project is easy to shoot and postproduce. However, don't stop now. If you have prepared carefully, you have a fine set of storyboards, a crafted script, and a list of equipment and locations. Now you need to execute the project efficiently.

Because your storyboards are unique, we can't walk you through the shooting process. However, here are some practices that will help as you shoot the raw footage.

1. Take your storyboards with you. Abandoning your storyboards now is like throwing away the road map as you pull out of the driveway for your cross-country trip.

2. Check/adjust the camera white balance for each shot. One off-color shot can drop a video project down a notch. Most camcorders have a three-way setting—indoor, outdoor, and automatic. Use the automatic setting when the light is coming from a mixed or undetermined source. For example, in the principal's office, light may be coming from an open window (outdoor) *and* the overhead fluorescent lights (indoor). The automatic setting allows the camcorder to monitor the light source electronically and make minor adjustments.

3. Consider taking a color monitor or television to the more involved indoor shoots. The monitor/television can be mounted onto a media cart. Seeing your work on a big color screen instead of the small black-and-white camera viewfinder can help your shot composition. Also, the monitor/television will allow you to play your recorded footage *before* you leave the location. If a problem arises, you can immediately correct it.

4. Employ some professional videotape practices. In chapter 6, we discuss buying "short loads"—10-, 20-, and 30-minute tapes—from a professional videotape supplier. It would be a good idea to use a different short tape for each location. This makes the editing process easier, and helps you avoid having to continuously search your single source tape.

    Also make sure you carefully label and log your video footage. Place a label on the face and spine of the videotape and indicate which shots/takes were the best. Don't forget to pop out the erase tab to avoid accidental erasure of your valuable raw footage.

Work diligently to shoot all of your raw footage. Review the composition tips presented in "Picture Composition" in chapter 1, follow the creative ideas planned in your storyboards, and make sure to label each tape as you use it. Once you have completed shooting the raw footage, you are ready to put your project together in the postproduction process.

Postproduction Activities

If you have completed the planning and production phases outlined above, you're ready to finish the project with postproduction. In this section, we'll discuss four areas of postproduction work: evaluating raw footage, using graphics, editing, and audio dubbing.

Evaluating the Raw Footage

After you have finished shooting your raw footage, compare it to the storyboard and make sure you have exactly what you need. Check for color (white balance), focus, and audio quality. If you are an experienced videographer, you will probably be very pleased with your raw footage. If this is one of your first video projects, you may find that you have to reshoot some of the scenes. Don't be afraid to reshoot. It is much easier to reshoot for a few minutes than to spend hours trying to edit poor footage into a good program, or explain to others why your program is really not as good as you would like!

If you are unable to determine the specific problem with any sub-par raw footage, ask a colleague with more video experience. Most teachers and media specialists are happy to help a fellow professional develop video skills.

Using Graphics

Graphics can make your orientation project more understandable and interesting. At the very least, you'll want to add a title and ending credits.

As you decide what graphics to use, and where to use them, keep in mind the following guidelines.

- Graphics should support and reinforce the video and audio. Don't use graphics to explain a topic. Graphics should be used to deepen understanding and reinforce verbal details.

- Graphics should not substitute for video. If you have a list of five important school rules, it might be very tempting to simply type title screens and show the graphics for 30 seconds each. Instead, show a student obeying the rule, followed by the graphic, and then perhaps the consequence of not following the rule. Never select graphics over raw video shooting.

- Make sure that your graphics are brief and concise. People watching a videotape will become quickly frustrated if they have to read a great deal of printed material on the screen. Try to summarize your message in a few words or a phrase. Don't type a paragraph on a graphic screen and expect your audience to read it.

You may also want to review the graphics section in chapter 1 beginning on page 46.

Creating Graphics Screens

Whether you're using handmade graphics or creating graphics with a character generator, there are a few simple composition rules to follow. Most of the concepts are covered in chapter 1, but we'll quickly review them here.

- Keep graphics simple. Overly decorative graphics may look pretty but can render the letters almost unreadable. Generally, a nice font (type style) on a one- or two-colored background works well.

- Use the one concept/one screen philosophy. Don't crowd a screen with long lists of information. Make the graphics big and bold. A well-received single thought is better than a poorly understood essay.

- Use high-contrast colors. Make sure that the viewer can clearly distinguish the lettering from the background. The best test for contrast is to turn the color knob all the way down on the television or monitor. Colors that truly contrast will contrast in black-and-white *and* in color. Avoid pastels on pastel backgrounds, and remember that some of your audience will be color blind.

- Make your graphics large enough so that they are easy to read. Ideally, the audience won't be sitting *too* far from the screen. However, some viewing conditions are less than optimal. If a large font is not available on your character generator, consider using one of the hand-drawn graphics methods.

- Make sure that your graphics match the reading level of your audience, as determined in the scripting process. This is especially important in the elementary school setting, as many new readers may be watching your program.

Titles and Credits

Because the title screen and the credits will be the first and last things the viewer sees, they will have a profound effect on the audience's perception of your program.

The Title. When creating a title screen, try to think of a creative way to make graphics that will draw your audience into your program without overwhelming them. One of the creative handmade graphics techniques described in chapter 1 could work quite well. In the absence of such a technique, begin with a simple graphic on a bold background. You may have the technology to superimpose the graphic over a rolling video shot. This can also draw an audience into the program. Remember, your audience will form opinions about your program as soon as your opening appears on the screen. Create a good impression with a solid opening.

Credits. The best rule for credits is "Keep It Simple." As the credits begin to roll, the audience expects (and is ready for) the program to be over. Don't expect an audience to maintain attention through a long ending credits sequence. If you have done all of the work on the project, a simple "Produced by. . ." credit, along with the date, may be sufficient. People who helped with the project can be rewarded with a nice thank-you note; a credit is not really necessary. Although five minutes' worth of credits may be expected with a two-hour movie, it doesn't really fit a seven-minute orientation tape. And how many times does the audience sit through the credits of a motion picture?

Carefully selected and created graphics can add to the effectiveness of your orientation tape. Follow the guidelines of graphic selection, composition, and creation listed above to make your program educational as well as enjoyable.

Editing

Once you have created and recorded your graphics screens, you are ready to edit your tape into a final product. Remember that when you edit, you are crafting the raw footage into a finished product. Editing is creating through deleting and rearranging, not saving and salvaging through slashing!

In this section we'll define video editing, review deck-to-deck and industrial editing, and discuss ways to edit to control the pace of your video.

What Is Editing?

Editing is the process of combining and rearranging videotape segments into a coherent program. In order to understand how this task is accomplished, you have to know how videotape is recorded.

Videotape passes across spinning magnets called audio and video heads at a rate of $1\frac{5}{16}$ inches per second. Over an hour's time span, almost 94 feet of videotape is recorded by the audio and video heads. The VCR heads actually erase and magnetize the videotape as it runs through the head assembly. Depending on the VCR, either three or four tracks, or areas of information, are recorded on the tape. The audio track or tracks are recorded along the top of the videotape. If you are using a stereo VCR or camcorder, the tracks are split; a monaural VCR or camcorder uses the same space to record only one track. The next area of the tape stores the video track—the picture of the videotape. Finally, a control track is recorded along the bottom of the tape. The control track tells the VCR and television when to begin a new frame of video. The control track is recorded in a series of electronic pulses that are read by the VCR and serve to stabilize the signal.

Why is it important to get so technical? Because there are two types of editing—assemble editing and insert editing—and they use different tracks on the videotape. As we discuss videotape editing, keep in mind that videotape cannot be cut and spliced together like motion picture film or audiotape. Doing so would break the control track's sequence, causing the picture to roll and shimmy for a few seconds after each edit. (Of course, the tape and glue would ruin the delicate video and audio heads, but that's beside the point.) Instead, editing usually involves making a copy, transferring the magnetic signal from one tape to another. Keep this concept in mind as we discuss assemble and insert editing.

Assemble Editing

Assemble editing is the process of editing the video track, the audio tracks, and the control tracks in consecutive order (fig. 5.4 on page 94). When assemble editing, we are taking all of the information on the source tape and recording it onto the finished project. Because we are copying the control track as well as the audio and video tracks, we must edit in sequence. In assemble editing, you can't go back and put a scene *before* another scene. The result would be a video "glitch"—a distortion in the picture—that would last about five seconds, ruining any video footage that

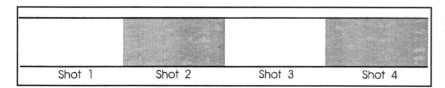

Fig. 5.4. Assemble editing mode.

had been edited afterward. Assemble editing is usually sufficient for most video productions at the elementary school level. Consult your storyboards, find the completed shots on the raw footage tapes, and assemble the project in sequence.

Insert Editing

The other type of editing is called insert editing. Insert editing allows the producer to select audio and/or video to be edited (fig. 5.5). In insert editing, the control track is neither created nor erased. Confused? Let's work through an editing example. Imagine that you are creating a brief documentary about the school's kickball

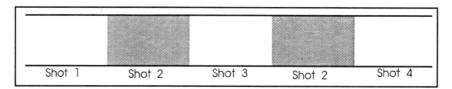

Fig. 5.5. Insert editing mode.

tournament. Your project has four parts: (1) shots of students playing kickball, (2) an interview with the coach describing the tournament, (3) a comment by a student about why she likes kickball, and (4) a shot of the championship team accepting the trophy. These four pieces can easily be assembled to create a nice segment for a news show. However, as you watch the segment, your attention starts to drift as the coach describes the tournament. Everything the coach is saying is important, so you don't want to edit any of it. However, the continuous close-up of the coach is boring. This is where insert editing comes in. In the insert mode, you can insert video without the audio. In our case, we video insert two shots of the student playing the game. Using this method, the coach's comments remain on the tape, but the segment is more visually appealing because we see the activity that the coach is describing.

Deck-to-Deck Editing

As you can imagine, there are many types of editing equipment. Television studios and stations use professional editing systems that cost tens—even hundreds—of thousands of dollars. Thankfully, all editing systems aren't nearly that expensive. In fact, you can probably configure an editing system with the equipment you now have in school. The system we will describe here is called a deck-to-deck editing system—a system that can perform simple assemble edits.

Two simple rules apply with this system.

Rule #1: Use four-head VCRs when possible. This allows clear still-frame tape cuing and smoother edits.

Rule #2: Use only shielded cable in connecting these machines. This will give much cleaner tape-to-tape transfer.

To connect a simple deck-to-deck editing system, you need two VCRs, two televisions, and four or five lengths of shielded cable with connectors to fit your equipment. This connection is actually quite simple, so we'll break it into two parts: connecting the VCRs to each other and connecting televisions and monitors (fig. 5.6).

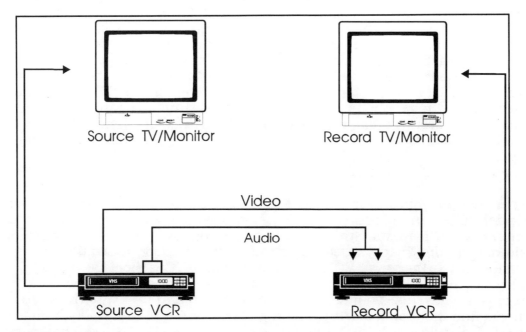

Fig. 5.6. Deck-to-deck editing connections.

Connecting the VCRs to Each Other. Set your VCRs on a table either side-by-side or, if ventilation is available, on top of one another. The left VCR, or top VCR, will be your source (play) VCR; the right VCR, or bottom VCR, will be your record VCR. This positioning is standard in the industry and will avoid confusion if you have the opportunity to edit at another facility.

Next, locate the "video out" and "video in" jacks of your VCRs. Run a length of shielded cable from the "video out" jack of your source VCR to the "video in" jack of your record VCR. Your video connection is now complete.

Now, locate the "audio in" and "audio out" jacks on the back of the VCRs. Run a length of shielded cable from the "audio out" jack of your source VCR to the "audio in" jack of your record VCR. If you are using stereo VCRs, there will be two sets of audio jacks, color-coded for left and right channels. Your audio connection is now complete.

Connecting the VCRs to Monitors or Televisions. Now the only connection left is to connect televisions to the VCRs so that you can see the video being played/recorded. Connect a television to the "RF out" of each VCR. (This will output video as well as audio.) How can you tell if your system is connected properly? A tape played in the source VCR should play through on both monitors/televisions.

Beginning the Deck-to-Deck Editing Process. The system that you have just created is called a deck-to-deck editing system, because you are editing from one VCR to another without the aid of an editing control unit.

Remember that videotape cannot be cut and spliced together like film. In order to combine and rearrange scenes, you must make a duplicate of the tape, copying the scenes in the correct order.

First, load the tape onto which you want to edit into the record VCR (right or bottom). This tape should be blank, or at least have a few minutes of blank tape left on it. Remember: You *cannot* edit a scene *before* another scene. This will destroy the control track.

It is nice to have a few seconds of black or neutral screen before your program begins. But blank videotape is not black and silent; it is snowy and filled with "white noise." So our first edit, then, will consist of adding this "black." You will need to obtain or create a "black tape." A black tape is a videotape onto which a black screen has been recorded with no sound. To create a black tape, record a videotape in a camera or camcorder with the lens cap on, the iris closed, or the camera pointed at a piece of black material hanging on the wall. To eliminate the sound, attach an adapter, but no microphone, to the mic jack of your camcorder. If you have a character generator, you can record a black screen. A black tape is usually kept at the editing station for this purpose. Pull out the erase tab so that no one can record on the black tape.

Load the black tape into the source (left or top) VCR. Now each VCR has a videotape loaded. By using the record VCR controls, find the place that you want to begin creating your new program. Put the record VCR on "record" and "pause." Now, push "play" on the source VCR to begin playing the black tape. Push "pause" on the record VCR to start the recording tape rolling. Both televisions/monitors should display the "black" video. After you have recorded 15 or 20 seconds of the black tape, *pause* the *record* VCR, then *stop* the *play* VCR. Eject the black tape from the play VCR while leaving the record VCR on "record/pause." Now find the first scene of your video (use your storyboards!) and load that tape into the source VCR. When you find the proper starting point, put the source VCR on "play/pause"; your record VCR should still be on "record/pause." (Note: Most VCRs will hold a tape on pause for only a few minutes. Until you master the deck-to-deck editing technique, your record VCR may automatically stop while you are cuing your next scene. You *must* recue the record tape if it turns off automatically. Pushing "record/play" again is not enough. Even an inch of blank tape can ruin 10 seconds of the edited project.) Now both VCRs are on their respective play or record and on pause. Now you must un-pause both VCRs to get the tapes rolling. But which VCR is rolled first? The *source* or *play* VCR must be un-paused *slightly* before the record VCR to ensure the recording of rolling tape. If the record VCR rolls before the play VCR, you will be recording a second of still frame. This technique may be desirable, but at this point it is an error. After the segment that you wish to edit is complete, pause the *record* VCR, then the play VCR. Once again, this will ensure that you do not record a paused image. Now you have completed your first edit! Load/cue your next scene and get to work. When your program is complete, run more black so that your viewer will not be exposed to the flash and loud noise of blank tape after the program is finished.

What happens if you allow more of your source video to be recorded than you intended? You need to recue your record tape so that the unintended segment will be recorded over on your next edit.

Let's review the procedure for a deck-to-deck edit:

1. Place the source tape in the play VCR and the tape onto which you will be recording into the record VCR.

2. Cue each tape.

3. Put the source tape on play/pause and the record tape on record/pause.

4. Un-pause the source VCR, and then un-pause the record VCR.

5. Allow the segment to be recorded.

6. Pause the record VCR, then pause or stop the play VCR.

7. Leave the record VCR on "record/pause." Find your next scene on the source VCR.

8. Repeat the process for each subsequent scene.

Here are some deck-to-deck editing tips.

• Log each source tape that you use. Write down each shot and its approximate length.

• If possible, use a separate tape for graphics and each scene that you record. This will eliminate much of your rewinding and fast-forwarding. For example, our school orientation tape may contain scenes shot in front of the school, interviews with the principal, interviews with teachers and students, and various shots around school. It would be easier to be able to use several raw footage tapes.

• Become adept at using your VCR's "search" functions. They will help you quickly locate shots.

• Be patient. It takes a few edits to master the technique. Before long you will be editing like a pro!

Industrial Editing

If your school is heavily involved in video production, or if you have made arrangements to edit at a high school, you may have the opportunity to edit on industrial video equipment. The main difference between deck-to-deck editing and industrial editing is the use of an editing control unit (ECU). An ECU is actually a microprocessor that can execute editing commands. The preliminary process for industrial editing is similar to the deck-to-deck process—both tapes are cued to their respective starting points. In the industrial process, a button is pressed and the ECU stores that location. Then the desired ending point is found, and another button is pushed. Then by pressing the "edit" button, the ECU takes over control of the VCRs and performs the edit with pinpoint frame accuracy.

Although the deck-to-deck process allows only assemble edits, the industrial system allows for insert editing as well. Another advantage of the industrial system is the ability to operate remotely the VCRs via a jog/shuttle control. This control makes cuing tape to proper spots quick and simple.

The biggest disadvantage of the industrial system is cost. Consumer VCRs do not accommodate an editing control unit. Currently, the least expensive industrial editing system on the market sells for about $3,000, which may be out of the reach of most elementary schools. However, many district offices, high schools, and middle schools have or can make these systems available. If you have deck-to-deck experience, you can learn to use the ECU very quickly. But beware: Once you have experienced industrial editing, you may never go back to deck-to-deck!

Controlling the Pace of the Program

Be very sensitive to the pacing of your program. Don't let any shot stay on the screen so long that your audience becomes distracted or bored. Even if the tone of your program is serious and formal, you still need to keep your audience interested. Show your edited footage to a few colleagues and watch their behavior as they view the program. If they squirm or begin to talk during longer shots, consider reassembling or adding inserts to quicken the program's pace.

Audio Dubbing

Audio dubbing means erasing existing audio track(s) on your program and replacing them with new audio. Audio dubbing allows you to add music and narration to appropriate parts of your program after you have edited the program.

Reviewing the Script

- Review your script in light of your editing and revise the script to make any necessary adjustments. A good script will augment and reinforce the video; a poor script will overwhelm and confuse.

- Guide the viewer through the program using the script. The narrator should provide a friendly/helpful tone.

- Use the script to provide a fresh perspective on the video. Avoid "Here you see. . . ." Make the viewer an active participant.

- Use the script to explain any activities that are not clear in the video.

- Practice reading the script to achieve the appropriate amount of script. Too much is overwhelming; too little leaves the viewer with a feeling of abandonment.

- Don't add useless or trivial information. Stay focused. Remember, the topic may be entirely new to the viewer.

- Write the script in the appropriate style. Some topics require a formal treatment while others can use a casual tone.

Connecting the Equipment

Here's what you need to perform an audio dub: a VCR that has audio-dubbing capability, an audio mixer, a unidirectional microphone, a microphone stand (desk or floor), a CD or cassette player, and two sets of audio patch cables.

Connect the music source and the microphone into their respective inputs in the audio mixer. (The unidirectional microphone eliminates unwanted noise from the surrounding environment.) Then connect the output of the audio mixer to the inputs on the VCR. Your simple connection is complete. To test your connections, connect the VCR to a television. Slowly turn up the volume on the television while you speak into the microphone and play some music. You should hear the voice and music through the television's speaker. Note: Make sure to adjust the audio mixer before testing the system. If the mixer's fader bars are at zero, no sound will go to the VCR or the television.

Performing the Audio Dub

When you are ready to begin the audio dub process, cue the tape to the first part of the program to be dubbed, and put the tape on "play/pause." Push the "audio dub" button on the VCR. The display on the VCR will shift to "audio dub/pause." This setting will allow you to adjust your music and voice before the actual dubbing begins. Play your music selection and read your script. Adjust the audio levels on the audio mixer so that the VU (volume unit) meters approach the red, but don't go into it. The VU meters measure the intensity of the audio. Too low, and the audio can't be heard; too high, and the sound will be distorted. After you have set your levels, recue the music, take a deep breath, and begin the process by un-pausing the VCR, starting your music, and reading the script.

Did you use "live" on-camera sound, such as interviews, during your program? *Do not* audio dub over that sound. It will be erased. *Before you begin* your audio dub, play your tape through and note the counter number when your live sound begins. *Stop* the audio-dubbing VCR when that number approaches. Then resume your audio dub at the next section. Audio-dubbing erases the existing audio track. And once it's gone, it's gone!

Music and Copyright

If you want to use music in your program, you must have the permission of the writer, composer, arranger, publisher, and all performers. Not obtaining this permission (and paying any royalties) is a violation of copyright law. Fortunately, an alternative exists. Professional-quality music is produced by production music companies, who in turn sell the rights to use the music to businesses, schools, and television stations for a fee. Your school district has probably purchased some of this music to use in productions like you're making. If not, contact your district media specialist and arrange for such a purchase. Media specialists are much happier when they're not in jail! Follow the copyright law and use music specifically designed for projects like yours, which your school or district has purchased.

Review

Let's review the steps to completing this school program:

1. Form ideas about the project.

2. Determine program objectives.

3. Procure funding for the project.

4. Determine the appropriate length for the program.

5. Determine existing resources that may have value to the production.

6. Write the script.

7. Create storyboards for the program.

8. Plan the shooting by making appointments and assembling needed equipment.

9. Shoot the raw footage.

10. Evaluate the raw footage, and reshoot any segments that do not meet your standards.

11. Prepare electronic and/or handmade graphics, including titles and credits.

12. Edit the raw footage.

13. Show the program to colleagues to determine if the pacing is correct.

14. Review and evaluate the script in terms of the edited project.

15. Audio dub the appropriate parts of the program.

Following these steps can contribute to a successful and rewarding production experience, and being able to produce such a project further validates the importance of video production in the elementary and middle school setting.

6 | SCHOOL-VENDOR RELATIONSHIPS

Schools active in video production will undoubtedly find themselves in the position of needing to purchase equipment from businesses in the community, either to replace broken, stolen, or obsolete equipment, or simply to augment the school's television production capabilities. Whatever the reason, the school enters into a relationship with a profit-centered business. Even though the business may provide attractive catalogs, beautiful showrooms, and friendly salespeople, their bottom line is their bottom line—the profit they will make from the sale.

There's no question that vendors can provide helpful, loyal service to schools; in fact, many vendors let schools know about exceptional values in the market and give special "school prices" upon request. Nevertheless, it is up to the school representative to enter this *business* relationship with critical listening skills, good questioning skills, and a real vision of the needs and direction of the television production program at your school.

In contemplating any video purchase, remember that the only reason you should ever buy an item of equipment for your school's television production program is because a real need exists and the benefits gained are significant. For example, the purchase of a small character generator would probably be a good idea for an elementary school video production system. Adding graphics to programs greatly increases the amount of learning and retention derived from the program. On the other hand, the purchase of an expensive computer-based graphics system, complete with paint-box, animation, and special digital effects, is probably unwise for the same elementary school, but might be appropriate for a well-funded middle school program. Although it is important to buy *enough*, it is just as important to avoid buying more than you can realistically use.

Equipment Purchases

Video equipment will probably be one of the largest single-item expenditures in your school. If you order a book that really doesn't fit into your collection, you've only lost a few dollars. You may even be able to return it for credit. However, a single camcorder, audio mixer, or character generator can represent hundreds of dollars and a significant portion of your A/V budget. For this reason, it is important to carefully evaluate your television production equipment needs before making *any* purchase.

Contacting the District Office

Your first step when contemplating an equipment expenditure should be to contact your district office. (Involve your principal, too. Most principals like to stay informed.) The results garnered from this communication will greatly depend on the media services offered in your district. If you work in a large school district that is firmly committed to technology in education, you may be able to speak with an administrative employee whose sole responsibility is to coordinate all television production in the district. If you work in a smaller district, your only advisor may be the district media specialist or the media specialist at another school who also has county administrative duties. This contact could lead in several possible directions. Let's use an example to make the point clearer: A middle school media specialist has decided to buy another camcorder to use in the student announcement show, and for teachers to use in classroom demonstrations. A district contact may reveal that the middle school is actually supposed to have the second camcorder, but for some reason the school just didn't get its unit. The district administrator may also be aware of some slightly used surplus equipment available in the district. Perhaps a high school television production department has decided to purchase a new camcorder and has no use for the old one. The district administrator could probably arrange for the transfer. Another possibility is that the district contact will tell you about a county bid list. Via purchasing bids, counties and local vendors frequently agree upon established prices for projector bulbs, blank tape, and filmstrip projectors. Those same bids often include camcorders and VCRs. The bid price is usually much lower than the retail price that a single school could negotiate. Even if there is no bid price on the item of equipment you desire, the district contact could initiate such a bid, thus providing a service to the entire district. The result would be that the middle school's camcorder could be purchased from the bid list at a very reasonable price. Finally, the district contact may be able to provide the media specialist with the name of a business that has worked with schools in the past and has a very good reputation. So, the best-case scenario has our middle school media specialist getting a new camcorder at no cost! At the very least the contact can provide the name of a local vendor who works with schools to satisfy everyone involved.

Another helpful by-product of the contact with the district administrator is to alert the administrator of the needs of your program and your desire to integrate television production into your media program. Such "familiarity" can lead to further profitable contacts. If nothing else, your purchase orders may get pushed through a little faster!

Keep in mind that in the equipment purchasing process, all knowledge is good. Don't be afraid to ask about equipment, qualifications, specifications, and vendor preferences. Keep a file of the information that you obtain. This information will help you make the best decision, and will allow you to assist colleagues who have the same questions.

Also remember that the customers can often tell you more about the business than the business itself. Ask potential vendors for the names of other schools and businesses that are on their customer list. Make some phone calls. Find out what the other schools think about the vendor.

Gathering Information About Prices and Practices

If you work in a small district or private school, or if your district media center decides not to pursue a bid on an item that you need to purchase, you may find it helpful to create an information-gathering process of your own, using the price information sheet presented in figure 6.1 on page 104. Although this form is not as polished as professional district-level forms, it will help you gather information on the product you would like to purchase. Note that this is not a bid. In many cases, a bid is legally binding; a school employee can get in serious trouble if the specifications of a bid are not followed to the letter. However, mailing a form like this to a list of potential vendors will establish you as a serious customer and allows the vendor to provide the information that is very important to you (fig. 6.2 on page 105).

Creating a Price-Information Sheet

In order to complete your own price-information sheet, you need to be a smart customer. Remember that you are the one asking for the price. Establish your own conditions that must be met. If the vendor cannot meet one of those conditions, then he or she may propose an alternative condition. Consider such alternatives.

Here are some items that you will probably want to include in your price-information request sheet.

1. *A detailed description of the item.* What features would you like to include? Look at the owner's manual for your current equipment, and list the features that are important to you. Also include the accessories that you expect. The lowest price may not include all of the items that you really want. Shop around. Visit vendors and learn about equipment. You can even go as far as stating "Camcorder—Panasonic AG-190U or similar." Let the vendor know that you know exactly what you want to buy. Also, don't forget to specify that you want *new* equipment.

2. *Payment method.* Specify the method under which you plan to pay. Must you provide a purchase order? Can you provide a school check at the time of delivery? Some vendors will price items lower if they know they won't have to bill a school or request payment on a county purchase order. Talk with your school or district bookkeeper. Although simply ordering from a purchase order may be easier on the media specialist, it may add a few dollars to the price. Also make sure the vendor knows that as a school, you do not pay sales tax.

3. *Warranty.* How long does this equipment need to be under warranty—90 days? Six months? A year? Does the warranty include parts, labor, and replacement of "lemons?" Do you need the vendor to provide a "loaner" while the item is being repaired? Determine the location of the repair facility. Will repairs be done at the vendor's shop, or will the equipment be sent on a slow boat to Tokyo? How the warranty clause is worded could greatly determine the speed of any warranty repair work.

4. *Delivery date.* How long are you willing to wait for the equipment? If you expect to have the equipment in your hands in two weeks, make sure to specify this point. You may be able to get a slightly lower price if you're willing to wait longer for the order.

Fig. 6.1. Information request sheet.

Information Request
Our school media department is considering the purchase of the equipment described below. THIS IS NOT A BID. It is simply a request for information that we will use in our purchase process. We will keep this information on file for future use and reference. Thank you.

School: Contact person:
School address:
School phone: (   )

Item description:

Accessories required:

Training and support requested:

Delivery date needed:
Delivery method:

Payment method:

Vendor Response
Vendor name: Phone number: (   )

Vendor address:

Name/model number of equipment:
Additional accessories included:

Warranty:

Site of any equipment repairs:

Price quote (including delivery method):
Price effective until:
                    Please return this form to the address above ASAP.

Fig. 6.2. Completed information request sheet.

Information Request

Our school media department is considering the purchase of the equipment described below. THIS IS NOT A BID. It is simply a request for information that we will use in our purchase process. We will keep this information on file for future use and reference. Thank you.

School: Pine Ridge Elementary **Contact person:**
School address: 123 Pine Branch Road, Limestone, Tennessee 01234
School phone: (123) 555-1234

Item description: VHS camcorder, multiple tape speed, automatic white balance, automatic iris, automatic focus, record-review, 10 x 1 power zoom lens (or stronger), manual iris control, manual focus, macro lens, microphone jack, headphone jack, audio and video outputs, installed microphone.
Accessories required: 2 batteries, battery charger/AC adapter, audio/video output-to-RF adapter, audio/video/RF cables, hard shell carrying case, complete instruction manual, lens cap.
Training and support requested: in-store explanation of feature access, telephone support when needed, in-store support when needed.
Delivery date needed: August 15, 1994.
Delivery method: Item must be delivered to the school. Vendor assumes all shipping liability.
Payment method: school purchase order; funds released upon delivery, check mailed within 10 working days.

Vendor Response

Vendor name: Phone number: ( )

Vendor address:

Name/model number of equipment:
Additional accessories included:

Warranty:

Site of any equipment repairs:

Price quote (including delivery method):
Price effective until:
Please return this form to the address above ASAP.

From *Television Production for Elementary Schools.* © 1994 Keith Kyker and Christopher Curchy
Libraries Unlimited, Inc., Englewood, CO 1-800-237-6124

5. *Delivery method.* Do you expect the item to be shipped, or are you willing to drive across town to pick it up? Shipping, insurance, and delivery charges can drive prices skyward. On the other hand, some larger items may require delivery.

6. *Training and support.* You may want to include a specification that you will receive training on the equipment. Although this request may inflate the price, it basically guarantees that you'll be able to work with the equipment the day that it is received. Would you like to be able to call the vendor with questions? If so, specify. The response to this request will help you gauge how the vendor views this transaction.

7. *Other information.* Always ask the vendor to provide any additional information about the product or his or her business. All of this information can help you make your decisions.

8. *A closing date.* Secure a date by which you will have the information you've requested. Do not wait weeks for a price. A vendor should be able to quickly and accurately provide a quote.

9. *A price quote.* Don't forget the obvious. Once you've obtained the price, you have a tailor-made purchase package!

If you already have a good relationship with a number of audiovisual vendors, you may want to use your information sheet as a tool for soliciting this information by telephone instead of through the mail.

Evaluating Your Responses

There is really no way to estimate the number of responses you will receive. Big retail chain stores may not be interested in providing for your needs. However, professional audio/video vendors are used to much stricter bids, and probably won't mind completing and returning your one-page form. The vendor may even follow up with a phone call.

Always make sure that you have received at least three completed information sheets. Making all of your purchases from a single vendor may be quite comfortable, but you should always check a competitor to make sure that everybody's pencil is sharp.

Examine all of the returned sheets carefully. Exceptions made by the vendor (for example, "battery not included") should be red-flagged for careful consideration. The lowest price is not always the best. Many other factors play into the school-vendor relationship.

Visiting the Vendor

After you have selected the price-information sheet that best fits your needs, pay an unannounced visit to the vendor. Talk with the vendor and find out exactly how he or she views this transaction. Ask several questions about the equipment to judge the vendor's reactions. If the vendor is impatient and reticent in answering your questions now, you should ask yourself if this is the person you want to be dependent on later, when you really need help. Ask for a demonstration of the equipment that you plan to purchase, but realize that if this visit is unannounced, you may have to schedule an appointment. Getting to know the vendor personally plays an important part in determining where you take your business.

Using a Box House

In slang terms, a *box house* is a vendor who sells video equipment while offering almost no support. Purchasing from a box house usually involves making your selections from a catalog, completing a form, paying on the spot, and walking out with the equipment under your arm, sealed in the shipping box. Many box houses only operate as mail-order businesses; they have no service-oriented sales staff or repair department. As you might imagine, box houses offer somewhat lower prices than many service-oriented businesses. Of course, some of your "savings" are recouped by the box house in the form of high postage and handling fees. Unfortunately, schools who buy from box houses find themselves without the professional network they need when a purchased item breaks or is defective. If you already know exactly what item of equipment you want and exactly how it works, and you already have several repair contacts in the area, you may want to investigate box house buying. However, if you covet professional service, face-to-face negotiation, and the ability to talk to a video professional instead of an answering service if a problem arises, you need to stick with local video vendors.

"Piecing Out" a System Versus System Pricing

Imagine that you've been awarded $500 to upgrade your school's A/V equipment. Because you already have three nice camcorders, and your instructional A/V equipment is holding up just fine, you decide to buy audio equipment that you can use on your school news show *and* with your school's PA system. You would like to purchase an audio mixer, two or three microphones, a cassette player, and a CD player. Your initial action might be to try to find the best price for each item of equipment. This approach is called "piecing out" the equipment. Although is sounds good, it can have *negative consequences*. When a system is pieced out, no vendor guarantees that the items are compatible. In our example of audio equipment, we would need to make sure the impedance of the systems match. Buying each item from a separate vendor implies no professional service or support. The equipment itself is only part of a professional purchase. The service and technical support is a valuable factor in the school-vendor relationship. The alternative is called "all or none" or "system" pricing. Using the system approach, a single vendor would provide all of the equipment, thus guaranteeing compatibility. The vendor would probably also show you how to connect the equipment to your existing television production and PA systems. Approaching a vendor with a system wish list will also garner recommendations of specific items of equipment. By taking the system approach, the vendor becomes part of the educational team, instead of just the equipment seller.

Pressure Sales

Anyone who has ever purchased a big-ticket item such as a car, boat, or home appliance has probably been subjected to a pressure sales pitch. Unfortunately, some video vendors apply this same pressure to their customers. Be very careful in such a situation. Buying video equipment is quite similar to buying a car. Like the automobile market, the video market has "model years." Equipment is updated annually and many items are discontinued. Therefore, a vendor with an inordinate amount of last year's equipment may pressure you into buying a specific model, even if it doesn't meet your specific needs. And unlike automobiles, video equipment usually offers more value in the new product lines. For example, last year's camcorder and the new model may be about the same price. However, the newer model probably has more features and updated technology. Is there anything wrong with buying "end-of-the-year close-out" video equipment ? No. Sometimes vendors are willing to make exceptional deals on equipment that they know will not be included in next year's product line. The trick is to make sure that *you, the customer* also know this. If the vendor can offer a substantial discount on the close-out merchandise, if the equipment meets your needs, and if the newer model doesn't represent a substantially better value, then purchasing the close-out camcorder can be a wise decision. But the pressure tactics must be put aside. *Always* be suspicious of a vendor who wants to push a specific item of equipment before knowing the specific needs of your program.

The Importance of Documentation

As you deal with vendors, keep a running log of your experiences. Write down specific dates and times of conversations. This log will come in handy if your equipment is defective or does not perform to standards. Write the equipment serial numbers in several locations (on the manual, in a file, etc.) in case the item is lost or stolen. Make a note of the purchase date in case the equipment is to be repaired under warranty.

Purchasing equipment from a vendor can be a mutually rewarding experience. However, the school representative must be aware of the specific needs of the school's media program and be able to verbalize those needs to a number of vendors to obtain the best value in terms of equipment, service, and repair. Establishing professional contact with vendors can lead to further educational exchanges for you and your students. As one media specialist stated: "I've learned more from my video vendor than from any instruction manual or journal article." Continually enlisting the service of professional video vendors adds more to your school's video production program.

Videotape Acquisition

Your school's video equipment probably represents a substantial investment. Therefore, you should be very careful about the quality of the videotape that you put into your camcorders and VCRs. Two factors come into play here: (1) the physical properties of the videotape, and (2) the picture quality.

Selecting a High-Quality Videotape

Videotape is a thin strip of plastic onto which metal oxide (rust) particles have been adhered. The entire tape is coated with a sealer that keeps the metal from flaking off the tape and into your VCR. The tape is then loaded into a plastic cassette shell and is ready for use. As you can see, the videotape manufacturing process involves several diverse raw materials. If the quality of any of these materials is substandard, the videotape will not perform to the desired specifications. A poor-quality plastic base may snap. Subpar metal particles will not properly record the image. A low-quality sealer will allow the metal oxide particles to flake off when the tape becomes warm through use, causing drop-outs on the picture. A subquality plastic shell will break the first time the tape is dropped. If you are recording valuable programs, store them on quality videotape.

Fortunately, many companies market high-quality videotapes that are easily available to the general public. A major label, blank two-hour tape can be purchased for $3 or $4 at discount stores, which usually offer discounts on quantities. Major-label manufacturers advertise on television and other media. Their products are available widely throughout the marketplace. These companies also have interests in photography, audiotape, and video equipment. Major-label tape usually costs only about a dollar or two more than store-brand counterparts, and the extra dollar is usually *very* well spent; generally, the premium grade offered by the major manufacturer offers better picture quality. Unfortunately, terms like "premium grade" and "superior quality" are thrown around like yesterday's laundry, and are quite subjective. Just because a tape says "superior quality" on the label doesn't make it so. Stick with the major name brands that let their company's most valuable asset—their good name—dominate the label and speak to the quality issue. A dollar saved at the checkout stand will come back to haunt the user in the form of broken tape and ruined programs. Remember, the majority of blank tapes sold are used for time-shifting—recording programs on a home VCR for later viewing. The fine details of picture quality are not that important to someone recording the late-show (or a teacher taping a favorite daytime drama). But a camcorder places much higher demands on a videotape, and a professional VCR tends to be much less forgiving of low-quality tapes. Spend that extra dollar on videotape when recording the school play or an important guest speaker—you'll be glad you did.

Blank Tape Dealers

If you are running a television production program in your school and purchase more than 50 videotapes a year, you should be buying your blank tape from a wholesale dealer, not a retail establishment. Blank tape dealers are usually mail-order companies that sell large lots of blank tape at greatly reduced prices. These dealers buy blank videotape—usually professional quality—on huge reels purchased directly from the manufacturer and load the tape into videocassettes. Consequently, a customer can order blank videotape of various lengths. Schools could purchase a number of these shorter tapes—for example, 30-minute tapes and 60-minute tapes—for special events. A guest speaker's presentation could probably fit on a 60-minute tape; a program of first-grade holiday carols on a 30-minute tape. The shorter loads allow you to record a single segment on a videotape. They also remove the temptation to continue using the tape throughout the school year, risking tape damage, theft, or loss; and as you've probably imagined, a short blank videotape is much less expensive than the two-hour version. If you haven't been contacted by one of these blank tape dealers, contact your school district office, another school involved in video production, or a local videotape duplicator for a recommendation. If all else fails, check the back of your professional video periodicals or go to the library and check the business pages of a big-city telephone book. Purchasing videotape from a blank tape dealer will save you money while allowing you to purchase videotape that meets the needs of your program.

As with equipment purchases, carefully check the credentials of the videotape vendor. Ask for the names of other satisfied customers. Determine the acceptability of a school purchase order before you place your order. Also determine any quantity discounts and purchase requirements before you decide to place an order. Some blank videotape dealers require a purchase of 50 tapes, while others will ship as few as 10. Remember, you are the customer. Make these vendors work for you!

Establishing vendor contacts in television production equipment and blank videotape sales is an important procedure for schools engaging in video production activities. Fortunately, once these contacts have been made, you have obtained more allies in your endeavors of education through media.

7 QUESTIONS FROM THE FLOOR

In the following pages, we'll try to answer some of the questions that we've been asked at conventions, seminars, and by visitors to our schools. Write to us in care of the publisher with your questions or comments.

I've seen advertisements for some pretty fancy television production equipment. In what order do I need to obtain this equipment?

Here is our equipment wish list. We believe that elementary and middle schools should obtain new equipment in this order:

1. a camcorder and a tripod

2. a hand-held and a lavaliere microphone

3. a high-quality industrial/professional VCR with monitor

4. necessary cable and adapters

5. an audio mixer capable of combining music sources and microphones

6. an industrial character generator with monitor

7. music sources (cassette deck, compact disc player)

8. a second camcorder, tripod, and microphone

9. a second high-quality industrial/professional VCR with monitor

10. an editing control unit

11. a video switcher

12. extra microphones (shotgun, PZM, etc.)

If you build your television production equipment collection in this order, you will be building a functional program using as little funding as possible.

How can I fund equipment purchases?

There are several ways to raise money to purchase equipment. One way is to approach the school PTA. The best time to approach the PTA is right after you have presented a PTA program on all of the great things you do with television production at your school. Tell them what you could do if you had just a little bit more equipment. Try to specify an item of equipment, and ask for the money to buy it. Rather than saying "I really need $150," say "Our students really need two tripods to continue learning about television production." Show them a copy of the list above, and tell them that you plan to build an exciting opportunity for the students.

A principal may be willing to make a small funding allocation for equipment purchases each year, particularly if he or she has seen positive results in the form of school video productions. Remind the principal of past accomplishments. Again and again. The squeaky wheel gets the grease, especially at budget time.

Don't be afraid to allocate book fair or other fund-raiser money to the purchase of video equipment. After all, video equipment is a valuable tool and just as important a medium as new magazines and encyclopedias.

Finally, find a friend in the school district office who will be on the lookout for other schools' discarded equipment. As high schools and vocational schools in your district update their television production equipment, they may have some older models that will meet your needs.

How should I repair my broken video equipment?

First, make sure the equipment is not covered by warranty. To make sure, call the district office. Sometimes districts require extended warranty periods for school purchases, meaning that an item that is a year old may still be under warranty.

Second, ask the district about its repair facilities. Most school districts contract with an audio/video repair facility for equipment service and repair. Let the district pay the bill.

As a last resort, take the equipment to a local, reputable vendor for on-site repair. Because this can be quite expensive, ask for an estimate before you run up a bill that will totally deplete your annual budget.

How can I gain the support of my administration and fellow faculty members?

The best way to gain the support of your administration is to provide valuable services to the school. Talk to your principal about producing a school orientation program. Provide an informative news show. Some people won't respond, but most will appreciate your efforts.

How should I respond to criticism of my television production activities?

First, determine the cause of the criticism. Some teachers and other school employees feel that television has no place in the school. It will be hard to win these people over. Try to point out the benefits of using television in the classroom. Sometimes people are critical because they feel left out of the process. Ask them to come in for a visit. Ask for their ideas, and be willing to incorporate their suggestions into your program. Realize that because television production activities are so visible they will likely result in strong feelings for or against the use of television technology in schools.

How can I learn more about television production?

There are several ways to learn more about television production technology. One way is to read more books like this one. Another is to network with other teachers and media specialists. Host a meeting to talk about video production activities. Ask everyone to bring a handout or idea used in their school programs, and a sample school news show. An hour later, you will have a number of new ideas. Also, attend school in-service meetings about television production. Consider attending meetings for middle and high school television production teachers. If your district does not host television production in-services, call you district media specialist and request one! Another way to increase your knowledge is to read magazines about video production. Start with consumer magazines found at newsstands and grocery stores. Progress to more professional publications recommended by high school television production instructors (several offer free subscriptions!). Visit your local audio/video vendor and ask questions. A good vendor enjoys the opportunity to spend a few minutes educating anyone who wants to learn. Your vendor can also tell you about (and perhaps provide free tickets to) audio and video trade shows where you can see firsthand demonstrations of new equipment. Finally, contact your local community college or vocational school about class opportunities. Many vocational schools now include television production as a course of study.

As you can see, there are many ways to educate yourself about audio and video production. They include networking with fellow teachers, attending in-services, reading television production periodicals, talking with your audio/video vendor, attending conventions and trade shows, and taking vocational or community college classes.

How can I create a news show set?

Many school news shows feature a student or students seated at an unadorned media table. To improve the set, cover the table with a tablecloth or some brightly colored paper. Decorate the wall behind the students with posters, student artwork, bulletin board paper, or even painted bed sheets. Use large machine- or hand-cut letters to spell the name of your show in the background. Add potted plants and a bookshelf with knickknacks to give your set a personal, lived-in look.

One of the biggest contributors to a visually unappealing set is the tendency to "overshoot" the talent. Make sure that you are providing close-ups and bust shots instead of long shots that show the entire student, dangling legs and all. If two or more students sit at the desk, make sure they are sitting close together. Studio talent should sit almost shoulder to shoulder, unless an appealing graphic or wall decoration hangs between the student anchors. Tightening the shot eliminates the need to decorate the entire set and allows you to concentrate on the few square feet surrounding the talent. Remember, you really don't have to create a set. A media center, office, or classroom can make a nice background.

We don't have a TV studio. What kind of room works best as a small TV studio?

Here are some considerations when selecting a room for use as a TV production mini-studio. The room should be quiet and "noise-controllable." The room should also be somewhat secluded from the rest of the classrooms. Students should not be able to walk into or through the television studio unsupervised. It's quite all right if only a few students know where the TV studio is.

The room selected as the TV studio should have a large number of electrical outlets; when using a complex television production setup, you will need up to a dozen power outlets. Even if you cannot imagine yourself making a multicamera news show, complete with graphics and segments, it's nice to be able to accommodate such a production if the need arises. Multiplying electrical outlets and running extension cords is inconvenient and potentially dangerous. It is much better to select a room that already has a number of electrical outlets available. The room should also be well lit. A bright room will make your video picture clearer and perhaps eliminate the need for extra lighting instruments.

Finally, your studio should be in a safe area where the equipment can be left standing from day to day if necessary. Student traffic through your TV studio could lead to injury and equipment damage.

In summary, your studio should be in a quiet, secluded place, free from regular traffic, with adequate amounts of electrical power and lighting.

Several parents are excited about their children's participation in the television production program. How can I get these excited parents involved?

Here are some ways in which parents have become involved in school television production programs:

- Parent volunteers can provide transportation for field trips.

- Parents can transport students to remote locations for off-campus shooting.

- Parents volunteers at school can supervise students shooting tape around the campus.

- Parents who are interested in video production can provide assistance in technical video tasks and maintain equipment.

- Parents can provide the names of friends who work in the television production industry who will visit as guest speakers.

- Visiting parents can be excellent interview subjects.

- Parents can help with set-building and decoration tasks.

Of course, make sure to follow all school and district guidelines when enlisting parental and volunteer support, especially as they relate to supervision and transportation of students.

What field trips would be good for students interested in television production?

Obviously, students interested in television production would like to visit a television station. Other opportunities include video production centers, tape duplicators, and high schools working in television production.

What about copyright law? How important is it? What laws do I need to be concerned about? Where can I go for help?

We often refer to copyright as "The Big C," not because it is the most important issue facing teachers and media specialists, but because it causes the most concern and results in the most questions. When we speak at workshops and conventions, copyright questions routinely take up a large portion of the question-and-answer period. People are concerned with obeying the law, which is good. However, so much information and misinformation has been circulated about copyright law that most teachers and media specialists are confused and befuddled. It doesn't help that interpretation of copyright law seems to be changing on a daily basis. Ten years ago, speakers were saying that using no more than 30 seconds of a song was legal; now the experts tell us to keep our paws off anything that has been copyrighted. Copyright concerns have invaded our music, our jewelry, our clothing, and even our favorite fragrances. As long as names, melodies, drawings, and designs are considered assets, copyright questions will exist. (Come to think of it, we would be pretty upset if someone photocopied chapters from this book and sold them!) Lawmakers contend that a complete copyright code would be too confusing and overly restrictive. So we rely on the experts to interpret proposed laws, court cases, and out-of-court settlements.

Our first piece of advice is to make yourself very familiar with your school district's copyright policy. We certainly advocate the authority of your employer to set guidelines for copyright use. If your district has no copyright policy in place, or if you feel that the policy doesn't address current audio and video issues, encourage your county administrators to adopt a policy for your use. In our opinion, interpretation of copyright guidelines is not the job of the building-level media specialist or teacher.

Second, consult a national authority on copyright policy. Perhaps the best-known authority is the Association for Information Media and Equipment, better known as AIME. AIME, a trade association for companies involved in production and distribution of informational film/video and equipment manufacturing has a mission that includes encouraging of good school copyright policies and educating schools and libraries on copyright law. AIME also pursues copyright violation reports and operates the Copyright Hotline, which answers questions about copyright policy and accepts information on copyright violations. By calling the Copyright Hotline, educators can request a copyright information packet, for a nominal charge to cover duplication and postage. The packet includes several valuable copyright resources and is a "must" for every school media center. In the past, we have found AIME quite helpful in answering our copyright questions.

So rather than reinvent the wheel and try to restate the copyright information that we've learned over the years, we'd like to refer you to your district office and AIME. The development of a legal, fair copyright policy is essential to every school district.

OK, I know you can't copy movies and charge admission. But what about music? Can I use music in my school orientation tape?

Sure. Music is a very important part of most video projects. But what type of music can be used? Obviously, you can't use a recorded, copyrighted tune in your video project unless you have the consent of everyone involved in the production *and* pay a hefty royalty fee. Because that process is probably out of the reach of most schools, let us explain a more reasonable alternative—production music. Several companies (at least 50) in the United States are engaged in the process of writing, performing, and recording music that is offered to video producers for use in their programs. The producer (that's you) purchases a cassette or compact disc of this music, usually for between $50 and $100. The collection typically includes seven or eight different tunes, and often contains several different versions of the same songs. (For example, a production music CD may contain a 4-minute, a 1-minute, a 30-second, and a 10-second [stinger] version of the same song; therefore, your CD will have about 30 or 40 cuts in all.) When you purchase this collection, you purchase the rights to use that music in audio and video production although you *can't* sell the music to someone else as production music. This is called a "buy-out," and represents an important investment for schools and districts. Using this music in your video programs ends the worry of violating music copyright when duplicating your tape. Most districts purchase a number of these cassettes or CDs for use at the district media center. Districtwide licenses can also be negotiated. Consult the district media center or professional video magazines for the names of production music companies. Most companies will provide a sample cassette, or send their latest volume on approval.

Part II
STUDENT CURRICULUM

NOTES FOR LESSON 1 HOW A VIDEO CAMERA WORKS

This activity is designed to teach students how a video camera works. It emphasizes the conversion of light and sound into electrical energy.

- Before handing out Activity 1

  1. Allow the students to look in the camera's viewfinder and see a picture being recorded.

  2. Connect the camera to a television/monitor. Allow the students to see and hear themselves on television. Ask them how they think the images and sounds are being recorded.

  3. Have the students stand in front of a mirror. Ask them how they think the images are being shown in the mirror.

- After the students have completed Activity 1

  1. Have the students locate and identify the parts of a video camera placed in front of them.

  2. Discuss answers to questions 2-5 on the student activity worksheet.

  3. Have the students share and discuss the pictures they made in response to question 6.

  4. Review the following terms:

     CCD chip   Lens
     Viewfinder   Electrical energy
     Sound waves

  5. Ask them why a mirror and a video camera are similar in the way they work.

Extension Activities

  1. Allow the students to record five minutes of their favorite school or classroom activity. Each student should replay their material in front of the group and discuss why he or she chose that activity to record.

  2. Allow the students to bring in videotapes from home that show them participating in activities at a much younger age. Not only are these fun to watch, but they can provide good discussion about the role of video and historical perspectives.

Answer Key

1.

microphone
viewfinder
lens
camera body

Photo courtesy of Panasonic.

2. b. Lens
   d. Viewfinder
   a. Body
   c. Microphone

3. b

4. c

5. Light is reflected off an object into the mirror. There it is turned back into an image in the glass.

6. Answers will vary.

LESSON 1: HOW A VIDEO CAMERA WORKS

Have you ever wondered how a video camera can "see" and "hear" a person or object? In order to understand how a camera works, you must first know the main parts of a video camera.

There are four main parts of a video camera: the lens, camera body, viewfinder, and microphone. Each part has a certain job to perform.

1. *The lens.* The lens of a camera is made of glass. It allows light to enter the camera body. The lens is the camera's "eye." It sees an image when light is reflected off an object.

2. *The camera body.* The camera body changes the light energy into electrical energy. When the light comes into the camera through the lens it hits a small computer chip inside the camera body. This is called a CCD chip. It is usually less than 1-inch square. This chip changes the light into electrical energy. This energy can now be sent into a television to make a picture!

3. *The viewfinder.* The viewfinder is a small television mounted on the video camera. The picture it presents is usually black and white. The videographer looks into the viewfinder to see what is being recorded.

4. *The microphone.* The microphone is used to record sound. The microphone "hears" the sound coming from an object and changes

A video camera and its four main parts. Photo courtesy of Panasonic.

the sound waves into electrical energy. This energy is changed back into sound when it is played on the television.

A video camera sees an object when light from the sun or another light source (such as a lamp) bounces off an object and goes into the camera lens. Have you ever looked at your reflection in a mirror? This reflection is really made from light that is bounced off your body and changed into a picture by the mirror. That's the same way a video camera works.

Light bounces or reflects off an object, goes into the camera lens, and is changed into electrical energy by the CCD chip in the camera body. You can look into the viewfinder and see the picture that your camera is recording.

A camera can "hear" and record sound by using its microphone. The microphone picks up the sound coming from an object and changes it into electrical energy. This energy becomes sound again when it is played on a television and the sound energy comes out of the television speaker.

A mirror image.

A video camera does not work by magic. It has to change light and sound into electrical energy. When this electrical energy is sent into a television, it becomes pictures and sound again. Now you know how a camera works!

From *Television Production for Elementary Schools.* © 1994 Keith Kyker and Christopher Curchy
Libraries Unlimited, Inc., Englewood, CO 1-800-237-6124

ACTIVITY 1: HOW A VIDEO CAMERA WORKS

1. Label the parts of this video camera.

   Lens   Camera body
   Viewfinder   Microphone

Photo courtesy of Panasonic.

2. Match the camera part to its job.

   _____ Lens   a. Changes light into electrical energy.
   _____ Viewfinder   b. Allows light to enter the camera body.
   _____ Camera body   c. Changes sound waves into electrical
                              energy.
   _____ Microphone   d. Shows you what your camera is recording.

3. What does a camera use to record an object?

   a. eyeglasses
   b. light
   c. sound waves
   d. viewfinder

4. What changes the light into electrical energy inside the camera body?

   a. lens
   b. microphone
   c. CCD chip
   d. viewfinder

5. Describe how a mirror works.

_____

_____

_____

6. Draw and color a picture you would like to record on a video camera.

NOTES FOR LESSON 2
HOW A TELEVISION
WORKS

This lesson is designed to teach students how a television works. It familiarizes students with the use of radio waves to transmit audio and video signals to the television, and it explains how these signals are converted into pictures and sound by the television.

- Before handing out Activity 2

  1. Turn on the television in the classroom. Ask the students to try to explain where the pictures and sound are coming from.

  2. Ask the students how they are receiving television signals at their home (antenna, cable, satellite).

- After the students have completed Activity 2

  1. Discuss the answers to questions 1-3 on the worksheet.

  2. Review the illustration in this lesson with the students. Discuss the functions of the following television components:

     a. electron gun
     b. shadow mask
     c. phosphor
     d. amplifier
     e. speaker

  3. Pass an RF (radio frequency) cord around the classroom. Allow the students to examine the copper wire used to conduct the audio and video signals. Demonstrate how to connect this cord to a television.

Extension Activities

1. Have the students make a list of the newest technological features on their televisions (remote controls, picture in a picture, stereo sound, etc.).

2. Obtain an old, discarded television from a television repair shop. Remove the back of the television and allow the students to view the components inside. You could even ask one of the repair shop owners or workers to come to your class as a guest speaker and talk about television components and repairing televisions as a career.

3. Have the students read about the history of television. Make a timeline on a bulletin board. Allow the students to select which historical events to

place on the timeline. This would make an interesting learning center for your classroom!

Answer Key

1. a. radio waves
   b. antenna, cable
   c. pictures, sound
   d. electron gun
   e. shadow mask
   f. phospors

2. a. antenna
   b. cable
   c. satellite

3. a. amplifier
   b. speakers

LESSON 2: HOW A TELEVISION WORKS

When you turn on your television, do you ever wonder how those pictures and sound appear? Where do they come from and how does your television make it possible for you to see and hear them? Let's find out how television signals are received and made into pictures and sound.

Your television receives the pictures and sound through the use of radio waves. Radio waves are broadcast by television stations and even radio stations all over the world. You can't see or feel radio waves, but they are being transmitted to your television (and radio) through an antenna or by a cable. Some people even use satellites to receive radio waves because they live very far from the television stations and there is no cable TV in their area.

Inside your television is a device known as an *electron gun*. This electron gun takes the video signal received by the antenna or cable and divides it into three colors: red, blue, and green. These color signals are then beamed at the back of the television screen. The screen has a row of dots or lines coated with a material called *phosphor*. The phosphor glows red, blue, or green when the signal from the electron gun strikes them. In between the electron gun and the back of the television screen is a sheet with many small holes, called a *shadow mask*. The shadow mask makes sure the beam from the electron gun reaches all of the areas of the television screen coated with the phosphor.

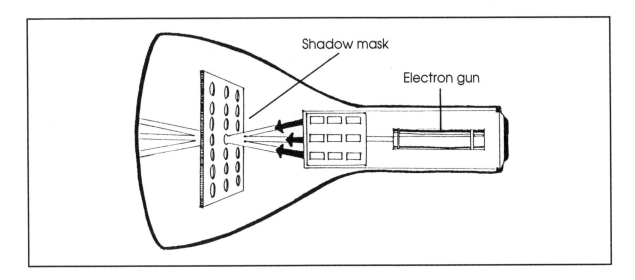

Shadow mask

Electron gun

The colored dots or lines of phosphor are so close together that they make a complete, full-color picture when seen from a distance. If you very briefly place your eye close to the television screen, you can actually see the individual dots or lines of the screen.

Now what about the television sound? Where does it come from? Remember that the radio waves carry both the video and audio (sound) signals. When the television receives those radio waves, it sends the sound signals to a small *amplifier* located in the television itself. The amplifier boosts the sound signal and plays it through a *speaker* in the television. Stereo televisions have two speakers, one for the right sound channel and one for the left sound channel.

Televisions are changing very fast with today's technology. Even now we can buy very small color televisions with screens as small as 2 inches. Or we can purchase large-screen televisions with screens as big as 5 feet! Some televisions allow you to watch two or more programs at the same time. People can also carry a television in their pocket or purse. What new developments will the future hold for television? Just wait and see!

ACTIVITY 2: HOW A TELEVISION WORKS

1. Use the following words to fill in the blanks.

   electron gun   shadow mask   phosphor
   radio waves   antenna   cable
   pictures   sound

   a. Television signals travel through the air as
   _____.

   b. These signals are received by the television using an
   _____ or by the use of a _____.

   c. The television changes these signals into _____
   and _____.

   d. Inside the television is an _____ _____ that
   beams red, blue, and green rays onto the television screen.

   e. The beams are shot through a screen called a
   _____ that makes sure the
   beam is directed to all parts of the television screen.

   f. The back of the television screen is coated with dots or lines
   made from _____ that glow red, blue, or green
   when struck by the electron beam.

2. List three things used to help televisions receive radio waves.

   a. _____

   b. _____

   c. _____

3. The sound in your television is made when the sound signal is played
   through these two devices.

   a. _____

   b. _____

NOTES:

NOTES FOR LESSON 3 HOW VIDEOTAPE WORKS

This activity is designed to teach students how video and audio signals are recorded on videotape. It explains that videotape is made of plastic and coated with iron oxide (metal). This metal coating can then be magnetized by electrical energy in the camera to record both audio and video signals.

- Before handing out Activity 3

  1. Show the students a bottle of iron filings and a magnet. Have them manipulate the iron filings with a magnet to make a picture. (There is a children's toy available in most department stores that uses this concept to allow children to add a beard, mustache, eyebrows, and hair to a picture of a man's face.)

  2. Allow the students to observe and handle a videocassette.

  3. Cut up pieces of an old videotape (about 24 inches in length) and allow students to feel, stretch, and manipulate the tape.

- After the students have completed Activity 3

  1. Discuss the answers to questions 1-5.

  2. Review the following terms:

     iron oxide   electrical signals
     audio track   magnetic force
     video track

  3. Have the students use a small plastic spoon or knife to actually scrape the coating of iron oxide off a piece of videotape.

Extension Activities

1. See if a local production or tape duplication facility would be willing to donate a sample of each of the following tape formats for your students to view and compare (½", ¾", VHS-C, Beta, 1", and 2").

2. Use a 9-volt battery, copper wire, and a nail to make an electromagnet. Use this device to manipulate metal objects (nails, screws, iron filings).

Answer Key

1.

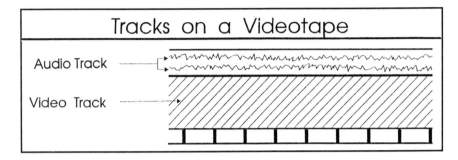

Tracks on a Videotape

Audio Track

Video Track

2. plastic
   iron oxide

3. magnetism

4. iron oxide

5. Answers will vary

Lesson 3: How Videotape Works

At one time or another everyone has probably played a videotape in a VCR. You may have wondered how the pictures and sound get recorded on the tape. No, it's not magic. Videotape is really made of plastic, and it is covered with iron oxide, a metal powder. The iron oxide coating is magnetized with the electrical energy from the video camera (picture) and the microphone (sound). These electrical signals are now recorded on the tape and can be made into pictures and sound when played back on the VCR and television.

How does this magnetic force work? Have you ever played with one of those toys that had a picture of a man's face covered with plastic and filled with small pieces of metal? You used a small magnet attached to a plastic wand to move the metal filings on the picture to make a beard, mustache, or even hair on the picture. Video cameras use magnetic energy to arrange the iron oxide (metal) particles on a videotape to record pictures and sound, much like that children's toy.

Videotape has a place for recording sound (audio) and a place for recording pictures (video). Below is a diagram of a VHS tape. Notice that the place to record audio is at the top, and the place to record video is at the bottom.

When the tape is played on the VCR, the electric signals recorded on

Magnetic drawing toy.

the videotape are changed back into pictures and sound by the television. So now you know that because of magnetic forces, the iron oxide (metal) coating on the tape can be used to record the electrical signals from a video camera!

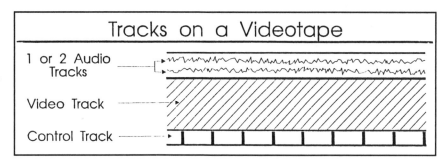

NOTES:

ACTIVITY 3: HOW VIDEOTAPE WORKS

1. Label this diagram of VHS videotape.

    Audio Track
    Video Track

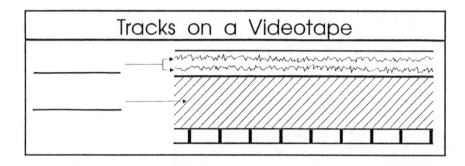

2. Videotape is made out of _____ and covered with a coat of _____.

3. What force is used to record video and audio on the iron oxide coating of the videotape?

    a. magnetism
    b. heat
    c. light
    d. sound

4. Of what substance is the magnetic coating on the videotape made?

    a. magnets
    b. iron oxide
    c. iron filings
    d. ironing boards

5. Draw and color a picture of a videocassette. Label it with the name of one of your favorite movies.

NOTES:

NOTES FOR LESSON 4
HOW A MICROPHONE
WORKS

This activity is designed to explain how microphones work. It teaches students that microphones use sound elements to change sound waves into electrical energy. The two main types of microphones discussed in this lesson are dynamic and condenser microphones.

- Before handing out Activity 4

  1. Place one or two microphones on a table. Allow the students to handle and inspect each microphone.

  2. Connect a microphone to a video camera or audio mixer. Allow the students to "hear" their voices as they speak into a microphone.

- After the students have completed Activity 4

  1. Discuss the answers to questions 1-6 on the worksheet.

  2. Have the students describe how each of the two types of microphones changes sound waves into electricity.

  3. Demonstrate how to connect the microphone into the video camera. If possible, record each student with a condenser (lavaliere) and a dynamic microphone (hand-held). Play back the videotape and allow them to compare the audio of each.

Extension Activities

1. Obtain broken or discarded microphones from a local news station or production facility. (Call some local high schools or even your district's media center!) Allow the students to take apart each microphone to see the sound elements. Have them identify the parts of each element and label the microphone as dynamic or condenser.

Answer Key

1. sound waves, electricity

2. dynamic, condenser

3. sound

4. a. condenser
   b. condensor
   c. dynamic
   d. dynamic
   e. condenser

5. Answers will vary.

6. Answers will vary.

LESSON 4: HOW A MICROPHONE WORKS

Sound, also called audio, is an important part of video production. Imagine trying to watch a news report or your favorite television show without sound. Recording someone's voice or the sounds of an event is just as important as recording the pictures of that event. Sound, or audio, helps the viewer understand what he or she is seeing.

Microphones are used to record sound on videotape. The sound waves are changed into an electrical signal by the microphone's sound element. This electrical signal is then recorded on the audio portion of the videotape. It can later be played back and amplified by a television.

There are two types of sound elements used in microphones for television production: dynamic and condenser.

Dynamic microphones use a magnet and a wire coil to change sound waves into electrical signals. The sound waves make the wire coil move and vibrate around the magnet. This vibration creates electricity, which travels through the microphone cord and is recorded on videotape.

Hand-held dynamic microphone. Photo courtesy of Shure Brothers, Inc.

Dynamic microphones are the most common type of microphone used in television production. They are very sturdy, have a good sound quality, and are not too expensive. Most schools use dynamic microphones for their student news reporting programs.

Condenser microphones use electricity (usually a battery) to change sound waves into electrical energy. A thin piece of metal or plastic is stretched tightly across a flat piece of metal or ceramic plate, called a backplate. When the sound waves enter the microphone, the metal or plastic strip vibrates. This vibration is turned into an electrical audio signal. The signal then travels through the microphone cord and is recorded on the videotape.

Condenser microphones are very sensitive to sound waves and produce a high-quality sound signal. Because they can be made very small, condenser microphones are often used for situations where the microphone needs to be kept out of sight of the viewer. News anchors often wear a condenser microphone clipped on their clothing when they are reporting the news from an anchor desk.

Because condenser microphones need power (electricity) to work, it is important to remember to have a charged battery available when using one.

From *Television Production for Elementary Schools.* © 1994 Keith Kyker and Christopher Curchy
Libraries Unlimited, Inc., Englewood, CO 1-800-237-6124

Condenser microphone.
Photo courtesy of Shure
Brothers, Inc.

You must also remember to turn the microphone "off" after using it so you do not drain all the power from the battery.

Although condenser and dynamic microphones have different types of sound elements, they both perform the same job: They change sound waves into electricity. This is the way microphones work.

ACTIVITY 4: HOW A MICROPHONE WORKS

1. A microphone works by changing _____ _____

   into _____.

2. The two main types of microphones are the _____

   and the _____ microphones.

3. Audio is another name for _____.

4. Use "condenser" or "dynamic" to answer each description:

   a. Uses electricity to change sound waves into electrical signals.

   _____

   b. Can be made very small. _____

   c. Very sturdy and inexpensive. _____

   d. Uses a wire and a magnet to change sound waves into

   electricity. _____

   e. Has excellent sound quality. _____

5. List two reasons for using a microphone for television production.

   a. _____

   b. _____

6. Draw a picture of a microphone used in your school for television production. Is it a condenser or a dynamic microphone?

From *Television Production for Elementary Schools.* © 1994 Keith Kyker and Christopher Curchy
Libraries Unlimited, Inc., Englewood, CO 1-800-237-6124

NOTES:

NOTES FOR LESSON 5
MANY DIFFERENT TYPES OF
MICROPHONES

This activity is designed to teach students about the wide variety of microphones used in television production. Students will learn about each type of microphone, its unique way of recording sound, and situations where each type of microphone should be used.

- Before handing out Activity 5

    1. Have a selection of microphones placed on a table for students to handle and observe.

    2. Discuss the following terms:
        a. directionality
        b. reflected sound
        c. transmitter
        d. lavaliere
        e. receiver

    3. Review the concept of how microphones work, as described in Lesson 4.

- After the students have completed Activity 5

    1. Discuss the answers to questions 1-4 on the worksheet.

    2. Have the students name and identify the microphones used at your school or in your television program.

    3. Demonstrate how each microphone is used. Show the students how to connect the microphone to the camera.

    4. Allow the students to practice connecting the microphones to the camera. Connect the camera to a monitor so the students can see and hear themselves using a variety of microphones.

Extension Activities

1. Students are always asking "How much does it cost?" Obtain a sales catalog from an audio vendor (Radio Shack, Shure, or any wholesaler) and have the students look up prices and model numbers for a variety of microphones.

2. Watch videotapes of local or national new reports. Have the students identify the type of microphone used in each report.

3. Take your video camera out to your playground or P.E. field, connect the wireless microphone, and see how far your reporter can move from your receiver before you start losing sound quality.

Answer Key

1. a. Surface mount microphone
    b. Lavaliere microphone
    c. Hand-held microphone
    d. Shotgun microphone
    e. Wireless microphone

2. Good sound quality
    Frees anchor's hands
    Easily hidden

3. They are very sturdy.
    They can be used by more than one person at a time.
    Not expensive.

4. Answers will vary.

LESSON 5: MANY DIFFERENT TYPES OF MICROPHONES

There are many ways in which microphones are used in television production. Reporters use them to introduce topics or to interview people. News anchors wear them when reporting the news at an anchor desk. Videographers use them to record the sound of events and activities around the community. For all of these different situations, a different style of microphone is used that best fits the camera crew's needs.

When choosing a microphone, ask yourself how it will be used during videotaping. Does the reporter need to hold the microphone? How many people need to use the microphone at a time? Does the microphone need to be kept out of the camera's view? Can the microphone be held or placed in a mic stand? Or will it need to be clipped to a person's clothing? Because there are many ways a microphone can be used, there are many different styles of microphones from which to choose.

The *hand-held microphone* is the most common style of microphone used in television production. Reporters use hand-held microphones for interviewing and electronic news gathering, or ENG, reporting. Hand-held microphones are very sturdy, can be used for more than one person at a time, and are not very expensive. Hand-held microphones should be positioned about 6-12 inches from the speaker's mouth; point the microphone at about a 45-degree angle.

Hand-held microphone. Photo courtesy of Shure Brothers, Inc.

The *lavaliere microphone* is very small and is usually clipped to a person's clothing. Because of their small size, lavaliere microphones are used in situations where the microphone should not be easily seen. They are often used by news anchors on a news show. Because the lavaliere microphone attaches to the anchor's clothing, it frees the hands, allowing the anchor to hold or demonstrate a product or activity.

Most lavaliere microphones are powered by a battery. They have excellent sound quality, but can only be used by one person at a time. They do not sound or look good for interviewing!

A lavaliere microphone should be positioned 6-8 inches below the speaker's chin. Be careful not to

Lavaliere microphone.

place the microphone under loose clothing. Otherwise it will produce unwanted sounds as the clothing rubs against the microphone.

Shotgun microphone.

The *shotgun microphone* is a long, tube like microphone used to record sounds from a small area. It can be "aimed" at a sound source to pick up those sounds from a distance. This makes the shotgun microphone ideal for videotaping scenes in which the microphone needs to stay out of view. Shotgun microphones are also useful for recording events, like sports activities, where the videographer has to stand at a distance from the action. They can pick up sounds quite well from the sidelines or the bleachers.

Shotgun microphones have a very directional pickup pattern. They can record sounds very well in front of the microphone, while at the same time blocking out sounds from the sides. Hold the microphone slightly above or below the sound source and point the microphone at the sound you wish to record.

You must be careful when handling a shotgun microphone because it will pick up the sound of your hands if not held firmly; many shotgun microphones come with a handgrip for holding the microphone. If you are using a shotgun microphone outdoors, place a windscreen over the microphone to avoid wind noise. Windscreens are foam rubber covers that slide over the top of the microphone. Many shotgun microphones come with their own windscreen.

How a wireless microphone works.

A *wireless microphone* operates like a small radio station. The microphone can transmit a signal through the air. This signal is picked up by a receiver, which is connected to the video camera or audio mixer.

From *Television Production for Elementary Schools.* © 1994 Keith Kyker and Christopher Curchy
Libraries Unlimited, Inc., Englewood, CO 1-800-237-6124

Wireless microphones are used in situations where using microphone cable is a problem. If your camera is too far from the sound source for your microphone cable to reach it, a wireless microphone would assist you in recording that sound. It can also be helpful in situations where you cannot have a microphone cord or cable because it would be in the way of the activity.

A wireless microphone system can be used with a hand-held microphone or

Wireless microphone.

a lavaliere microphone. With a hand-held mic, the transmitter is located in the microphone handle. Lavaliere styles usually have a small transmitter that attaches to the user's belt or clothing. These transmitters need a battery to operate. Most wireless microphone receivers can operate on electric (AC) or battery power (DC). If you are using a wireless microphone system, read the owner's manual for distance guidelines. The farther the distance between the mic and receiver, the greater the chance for poor sound quality or interference. Also, because wireless microphones actually broadcast their signals, they can be interrupted by other electronic signals. For example, radio-controlled toys, walkie-talkies, cordless telephones, and other transmitted signals may interrupt your wireless microphone's sound.

Wireless microphones require some training to use them correctly. Once you have learned to correctly connect the microphone system to your camera or audio mixer, you can have fun using the wireless microphone for producing your videos!

The *surface mount microphone* is made to be placed on a flat surface, such as a table or desk. It picks up sounds that are reflected off the flat surface, using the surface to give it a stronger sound signal. Most surface mount microphones use a battery for power. Surface mount micro-

Surface mount microphone. Photo courtesy of Shure Brothers, Inc.

phones are excellent for recording sound from a group of people seated at a desk or table.

Because television production takes place in many different places and situations, you need to have different types of microphones for reporting these events. Learn to use many kinds of microphones so you will be able to choose the right microphone for the right situation!

NOTES:

ACTIVITY 5: MANY DIFFERENT TYPES OF MICROPHONES

1. Identify each microphone by its description.

   a. Usually placed on a table or desktop to pick up sound.

   _____

   b. Often clipped on the user's clothes. _____

   c. Most often used for interviewing at the scene. _____

   d. Can be aimed at the sound source and kept out of the camera frame while recording. _____

   e. Transmits sounds through the air to a receiver connected to the camera. _____

2. Why are lavaliere microphones so often used in television production?

   _____

   _____

   _____

3. List two reasons why hand-held microphones are good for ENG reporting.

   _____

   _____

4. List two videotaping activities where you would choose to use a shotgun microphone for recording sound.

   _____

   _____

NOTES:

NOTES FOR LESSON 6 CHOOSING THE RIGHT MICROPHONE

This lesson is designed to familiarize students with the selection of a microphone that best fits the videotaping situation. Students will be able to select from among the following microphones: hand-held, shotgun, lavaliere, wireless, and surface mount microphones.

- Before handing out Activity 6

  1. Allow the students to observe and handle a variety of microphones discussed in this chapter.

  2. Review how a microphone works and identify each type of microphone on display.

- After the students have completed Activity 6

  1. Discuss the answers to questions 1-10 on the worksheet. Several microphones could be used for some of the situations. Elicit responses that encourage students to state *why* they would choose each particular microphone.

  2. Demonstrate how to connect each style of microphone to the video camera.

  3. Videotape students using a variety of microphones around the school. Replay them in class and discuss how each type of microphone was used, why it was selected, and evaluate its performance for that situation.

Extension Activities

1. Allow the students to videotape several teachers instructing their classes to simulate the experience of videotaping a guest speaker. Use several different kinds of microphones. Compare videotaping sessions and have the students discuss microphone selection and sound quality.

2. Watch some videotaped portions of your local or national news shows. Have the students identify the style of microphones used and discuss why those microphones were chosen.

Answer Key

Answers may vary but should include . . .

1. lavaliere, shotgun
2. hand held, shotgun
3. shotgun
4. wireless, shotgun
5. lavaliere, wireless, shotgun
6. shotgun
7. shotgun
8. lavaliere, shotgun
9. shotgun
10. hand held

LESSON 6: CHOOSING THE RIGHT MICROPHONE

Choosing the best type of microphone to use for reporting or taping an event is an important skill in television production. Asking yourself how the microphone will be used or where it will be placed will help you decide which type of microphone to choose.

Interviewing with a hand-held microphone.

A hand-held microphone is most often used for interviewing. The reporter can hold the microphone and use it to record questions and answers during the interview. Hand-held microphones are used because you can interview one or several people at a time with just one microphone.

When you are using a hand-held microphone for interviewing, be sure to aim the microphone at the speaker's mouth and hold the microphone 6-8 inches below his or her chin. When you are asking a question, point the microphone at your mouth. Do not position the microphone so that it covers either the face or the mouth!

News Reporting

News reporting is most often done with a hand-held microphone. It can be used for reporter introductions and lead-outs, as well as "on-the-scene" interviews.

There are some special situations where a lavaliere microphone would be a better choice. When a reporter needs to hold or demonstrate an object, a lavaliere microphone frees the reporter's hands and still records the reporter's script. At a book fair, for example, the reporter could be holding up a book or two as the introduction is videotaped. Lavaliere microphones are often used for reporting news at an anchor desk. Because of their small size, they are not in the way of the camera. News anchors often need to hold scripts or announcements while reporting the news. A lavaliere microphone enables them to do just that!

During most sporting events, videographers and reporters must keep off the field. A shotgun microphone would be

used to record the sound of the event from the sidelines and bleachers because it is designed to pick up sounds from a distance. Shotgun microphones can be placed on the camera or held with a special handgrip.

Classroom Videotaping

School news reporting usually involves taping activities that happen in classrooms, hallways, and auditoriums. Most of the time the video camera's microphone will be fine for recording these events. However, there may be two situations where a different microphone could be used to get a better sound recording.

1. *Group discussions.* A surface mount microphone can be placed on a table or desk to record small group discussions. These microphones are made to record sound from all directions, so they would be ideal for taping reading groups, discussion groups, or similar activities.

2. *Guest speakers.* If you just want to record a few minutes of a guest speaker to show in a news report, your camera microphone would be fine to use. However, if you are recording the speaker for later use in other classes, your camera microphone would not be the best choice.

A lavaliere microphone clipped to the speaker's clothes would provide great sound, and the speaker would still be able to move around a little. A hand-held microphone placed in a microphone stand could also be used, but the speaker would not be free to move away from the mic. A shotgun microphone could also be used and would provide good sound for a question-and-answer session. However, it tends to pick up unwanted sounds (air conditioners, fans, desk and chair noises, etc.).

If the guest speaker is in an area where placing microphone cords is a problem, a wireless microphone should be used. Wireless microphones provide excellent sound quality and come in lavaliere or hand-held styles. A wireless microphone also provides your speaker with the ability to move freely around the room.

Choosing the right microphone for each videotaping situation is a result of training and experience. As you become more skilled in selecting and using different microphones, your video projects will look and sound better.

ACTIVITY 6: CHOOSING THE RIGHT MICROPHONE

Choose the best microphone for each videotaping situation.

| hand-held | wireless | surface mount |
| lavaliere | shotgun | |

1. You are holding a poster of a manatee while introducing your report on manatees.

   _____

2. You are interviewing three "Students of the Month" at your school.

   _____

3. You are videotaping a softball game between the fourth- and fifth-grade classes. You must sit in the bleachers behind first base.

   _____

4. You are videotaping a guest speaker on the stage in the auditorium. Your camera is placed in the back of the room.

   _____

5. You are reporting the news from your television studio's anchor desk.

   _____

6. You are videotaping four children seated around a table talking about their favorite poems.

   _____

7. You are videotaping a guest speaker in a classroom. There is a 15-minute question-and-answer session at the end of his talk.

   _____

8. You are reporting "at the scene" of this year's Science Fair. You are holding the first-place project.

   _____

9. You are videotaping a group presentation about recycling. The group is standing at the front of the classroom.

   _____

10. You are interviewing the principal about this week's book fair.

    _____

From *Television Production for Elementary Schools*. © 1994 Keith Kyker and Christopher Curchy
Libraries Unlimited, Inc., Englewood, CO 1-800-237-6124

NOTES:

NOTES FOR LESSON 7
TRIPODS

This activity is designed to familiarize students with the use of a tripod in television production. Tripods can be fitted with a wheeled base, called a dolly, which enables them to be easily moved from one position to another. Tripods and dollies can also be used to perform several camera shots such as pans, tilts, trucks, and dollies.

- Before handing out Activity 7

    1. Set up a tripod in the classroom. Allow the students to manipulate the head. If you have a dolly, attach it to the tripod.

    2. Discuss with your students why tripods are used in television production.

- After the students have completed Activity 7

    1. Discuss the answers to questions 1-5 on the worksheet.

    2. Assist the students in attaching the video camera to the tripod. Show them how to set up the tripod and mount the camera to the tripod head. Demonstrate how to move the camera from one position to another with the tripod on a dolly.

    3. Demonstrate the following camera shots:
       pan   tilt   dolly   truck

    4. Allow the students to practice the above camera shots. Discuss taping situations where these camera movements might be used.

Extension Activities

1. Visit a local news station. Observe their studio camera supports (called pedestals).

2. Watch one or two television shows, or even a video movie. Have students identify camera movements (pans, tilts, trucks, dollies) that are used in the show.

Answer Key

1. Provides a steady shot.
   Keeps videographer from getting tired and sore.

2. tripod head

3. dolly

4. quick release pin

5. a. dolly
   b. truck
   c. tilt
   d. pan

LESSON 7: TRIPODS

A tripod is a three-legged stand that holds and supports a video camera. Tripods help the videographer keep a steady shot for long periods of time. Imagine if you had to hold a video camera on your shoulder while taping a guest speaker! After a few minutes, your arms and shoulders would become very tired. The camera shot would become very shaky. That is why tripods are used in television production. Tripods do not get tired.

Tripods are also used for recording a few selected camera shots and angles. A shot called a "pan" is made by moving the camera to the left or right while recording. Moving the camera up or down while recording is called a "tilt" camera shot. Using a tripod for these camera shots will assist you in recording a smooth and steady shot.

There are several ways of attaching the video camera to a tripod. Some tripods have a screw that fits into the bottom of the video camera. You simply place the camera on the tripod "head" (the flat top part of the tripod) and turn the screw with your fingers until the camera is securely attached to the tripod head. Sometimes using this type of mounting device can be difficult and take a lot of time to accomplish. That is why many tripods use a "quick-release pin" to mount the camera on the tripod. The quick-release pin screws into the bottom of the video camera and can be quickly and easily snapped onto the head of the tripod. If you need to move the camera, it can be just as quickly removed from the tripod.

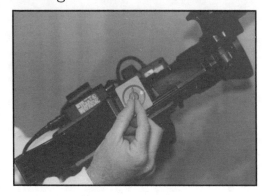

Quick-release pin.

When you are finished videotaping, it is best to place the quick-release pin back on the head of the tripod. Then you will always know where to find it the next time you need it.

Many tripods come equipped with wheels that attach to the legs of the tripod. This wheeled base is called a "dolly." This makes moving the camera from one place to another very easy. A dolly can also be used to record some special camera shots and angles. A camera shot recorded while wheeling the tripod toward the subject is called a "dolly in" camera shot. A camera shot recorded while wheeling the camera away from the subject is a "dolly out" or "dolly back." A camera shot recorded while moving the dolly to the left or right is called a "truck." A videographer may be called upon to record these type of camera shots for television programs or even movies!

As you can see, a tripod can provide two services: It can help you hold and support your camera and assist you in recording special camera shots like dollies and trucks.

ACTIVITY 7: TRIPODS

1. What are two reasons videographers use tripods?

   _____

   _____

2. What do we call the flat surface on the top of the tripod?

   _____

3. What do we call the wheeled base that fits on the legs of a tripod?

   _____

4. What do we call the mounting device on a tripod that lets us quickly attach or release a camera on a tripod?

   _____

5. Use the following camera terms to name each camera shot:

   dolly   pan   truck   tilt

   a. Rolling the camera forward or backward while recording.

   _____

   b. Rolling the camera left or right while recording.

   _____

   c. Moving the camera up or down while recording.

   _____

   d. Moving the camera left or right while recording.

   _____

NOTES:

NOTES FOR LESSON 8
THE THREE CS:
COMPOSITION, CLARITY, AND CONTINUITY

This activity is designed to teach students some aspects of picture composition, focusing techniques, and continuity that they can use in their video projects.

- Before handing out Activity 8

   1. Discuss and demonstrate the following terms:

Composition. Bring in a framed picture or photograph. Show the students how it is centered in the frame. Have them look at pictures in magazines and books. Discuss how they are framed.

Clarity. Put some sand in the bottom of a glass jar. Now fill it with water. Let it stand for a while so the sand settles at the bottom. Show the students the jar. Now shake it up. Discuss the idea of water clarity. Now relate it to a video picture.

Continuity. Cut out some comic strips (like Garfield or Peanuts) from the Sunday newspaper. Use a marker to change the colors of some of the clothes or characters. You can even mix scenes from different weeks in the same story. Let the students look at them and ask them what appears wrong with the strips. Point out the lack of continuity when one scene is different from another in the same story.

- After the students have completed Activity 8

   1. Discuss the answers to questions 1 and 2 on the worksheet.
   2. Connect your video camera to a monitor. Have the students practice framing a variety of shots.
   3. Connect your video camera to a monitor. Place several objects around the room. Switch your camera to manual focus. Let the students practice zooming in and focusing on the objects.
   4. Connect your video camera to a monitor. Let the students practice video-taping each other as they walk across the room (leadroom).
   5. Practice interviewing two or three students in one location and slightly changing the camera angle so the background is different in each interview. Review these in class and contrast them with interviews in which the camera does not move and the background remains the same in all of the interviews. Which approach works best? Why?

Extension Activities

1. Let the students practice their skills on the P.E. field. Try using composition skills (leadroom, headroom) as you try and videotape students running or playing basketball, soccer, or other sports. Bring the tape back to class and critique it.

2. Invite a local news videographer to speak with the students about composition, clarity, and continuity. Maybe he or she could also bring in some videotape that was shot for the news and point out these aspects as they watch the tape.

Answer Key

1. a. headroom
   b. focus ring
   c. leadroom
   d. continuity
   e. autofocus
   f. framing

2. 1. Switch to manual focus.
   2. Zoom to get a close-up of the subject.
   3. Turn the focus ring until the picture is sharp and clear.
   4. Zoom out to the shot.

LESSON 8: THE THREE CS: COMPOSITION, CLARITY, AND CONTINUITY

A videographer's camera is much like an artist's brush: It creates a picture that tells a message. Like an artist, the videographer must create a picture that is attractive to the viewer. It must be pleasant to look at and still tell the story of an event. Learning to use the "Three Cs" (composition, clarity, and continuity) is important for good videography.

Composition

Composition refers to how the videographer frames the picture to be recorded. Like a photograph in a picture frame, a videographer must be sure to frame the subject correctly in the camera's viewfinder.

You must leave some room at the top of the frame so the subject's head is not touching the top of the picture. This is called headroom. Try to keep the subject in the center of the picture, or frame.

If the subject of your shot is moving or walking, he or she should be framed so that there is room in front of him or her in the picture frame. This is called leadroom.

A person moving to the left or right should be framed so that two-thirds of the frame is in front of him or her. This prevents the subject from "bumping" into the side of the picture frame as he or

Headroom above subject.

Leadroom in front of subject.

she moves. It also lets the viewer see where the subject is moving to.

When shooting a close-up you will probably not include the subject's entire body. Be careful that you do not frame the shot in such a way that the person's head, waist, knees, or ankles are at the bottom edge of the screen. Instead, frame them so that these body parts are a little above or below the edge of the screen.

From *Television Production for Elementary Schools.* © 1994 Keith Kyker and Christopher Curchy Libraries Unlimited, Inc., Englewood, CO 1-800-237-6124

Clarity

Right and wrong ways to frame subjects.

Learning to videotape sharp, clear pictures is also important for good videography. There are two important camera operations that can help you achieve clarity: white-balancing and focusing.

White-balancing involves setting your camera to videotape in either outdoor light or indoor light. White-balancing your camera makes the colors of the recorded objects as realistic as possible. Most cameras have a switch that tells the camera if you are outdoors or indoors. These settings are either printed next to the white-balance switch, or they may be symbols (light bulb for indoors and a sun for outdoors). Make sure your camera is on the right setting each time you videotape.

Focusing your camera is also important for clarity. Most cameras have an automatic focus that uses an invisible beam of light to adjust the camera's focus as you videotape. However, if you move the camera while videotaping, the autofocus will take a few seconds to correct itself. During these few seconds your picture will be out of focus. If you can learn to focus the camera by yourself (manual focus), you will be able to avoid those few blurry shots as you videotape.

To manually focus your camera, first switch the camera from autofocus to manual focus. You can now focus the camera yourself by turning the camera's focus ring. The focus ring is located on the end of the camera lens. There are four easy steps for manually focusing your camera so that your picture remains sharp and clear, even if your subjects are moving around:

Step 1: Switch to manual focus.

Step 2: Zoom all the way in so that you have a good close-up of your subject.

Step 3: Turn the focus ring so that the picture is sharp and clear.

Step 4: Now zoom out to the shot you want to videotape. The picture will stay in focus no matter how far you zoom out or in to your subject.

Learning to manually focus your camera will take some practice. With more experience you will be focusing faster and videotaping a better-quality picture than by using the autofocus method.

Continuity

By achieving continuity—shooting people and events as they look and act normally—you will ensure that your video projects appear as real and true to life as possible. For example, you are videotaping a story about the third grade's field trip to the zoo. On Monday, you interview the teachers and students about their trip. Then on Tuesday you videotape a report about them writing stories and painting pictures about the animals they saw at the zoo. When you put these two parts of the project together, you will notice that you are wearing different clothes! Maybe your hair is fixed differently, too! No one will accept your video report as a single account because they can see that you did the interviews on different days. This is poor continuity. How could you have done this report in pieces and still kept good continuity? By wearing the same clothes both days (be sure to wash them each night!). That way the report would appear as if it had all been produced in one day. Look at movie stars. They must look the same throughout an entire movie even though it may take three to six months to complete! That is why makeup and wardrobe staff are on the set of every film. It is their job to make the actors and actresses look the same for all of the scenes even if they are filmed on different days.

Continuity problems can also result when we interview several people in the same location. The reporter and the background stay the same for each interview, but the guests seem to "magically" appear and disappear next to the reporter. Try to use a different camera angle for each interview so the background in the shot is a little different each time. This will make your projects more interesting and give them better continuity, too.

Good videography doesn't just happen overnight. It takes practice and experience. If you remember the three Cs of composition, clarity, and continuity, your projects will look better and be more interesting to watch.

NOTES:

ACTIVITY 8: THE THREE CS: COMPOSITION, CLARITY, AND CONTINUITY

1. Use these words to fill in the blanks.

   framing   leadroom   focus ring
   headroom   autofocus   continuity

   a. Leaving a little room between a person's head and the top of the screen is called _____.

   b. Located on a camera's lens, this is used to make the picture sharp and clear. _____

   c. Framing a moving person so that he or she does not "bump" into the edge of the screen is called _____.

   d. Wearing the same clothes while taping a project over two days is done to maintain _____.

   e. A camera uses an invisible beam to make the picture sharp and clear. This is called _____.

   f. Centering a subject in the viewfinder is called _____.

2. List the four steps you use to manually focus your video camera.

   1. _____

   _____

   2. _____

   _____

   3. _____

   _____

   4. _____

   _____

From *Television Production for Elementary Schools.* © 1994 Keith Kyker and Christopher Curchy
Libraries Unlimited, Inc., Englewood, CO 1-800-237-6124

NOTES:

NOTES FOR LESSON 9 WHERE DO THEY GET THE NEWS?

This activity is designed to teach students about the many sources of information available to news stations and reporters.

- Before handing out Activity 9

  1. Ask the students what type of stories they see on the local news. Make a list on the chalkboard. Help them categorize the stories (world, national, local).

  2. Videotape a local newscast. Watch it in class with your students. Identify the type of story as it is being viewed (world, national, local). Ask the students where they think the information and videotaped pictures came from for each event.

- After the students have completed Activity 9

  1. Review the answers to questions 1-10 on the worksheet.

  2. Review the following terms:

     a. bureau
     b. network
     c. stringer
     d. wire services
     e. news beat
     f. satellite
     g. press release

  3. Faxes have also become an important news source. If your school office has a fax machine, take the students to see how faxes are sent and received. Contrast the fax to the teletype.

Extension Activities

1. Have the students write a three-to-five sentence news report from an article in the daily newspaper. Have them list the types of camera shots they would want to use for their story as it was being read "on the air."

2. Visit a local news station. Ask a reporter to show the students the sources used at the station to get news information.

3. Have the students write their own press release. What information needs to be included?

4. Borrow or rent a police scanner to set up in your room. Let the students listen to the broadcast from the station. What type of code words and numbers do they hear? Why are codes used?

5. Invite a local police officer to come to the class to speak about the use of codes over the police radio.

Answer Key

1. Wire services
2. Police radio
3. Telephone
4. News beats
5. Newspaper
6. Networks
7. Tips
8. Stringers
9. News bureaus
10. Mail handouts

LESSON 9: WHERE DO THEY GET THE NEWS?

When viewers turn on the local TV news, they expect to see and hear stories about many different events and activities. They want to learn about things that have happened in the community, but they also expect to see news from around the state, nation, and even the world. How does your local news station get these reports and videotaped footage? Most news stations use many different sources for getting news.

Wire Services

Wire services keep news stations informed about events that happen all over the world. News stations receive this information over a teletype 24 hours a day. A teletype is like a typewriter and a telephone combined. It receives information from around the world and types it out in the newsroom. Reporters can read this information and use it to write news reports for their news show. News stations pay to use these wire services. The two largest wire services are the Associated Press (AP) and United Press International (UPI).

Networks

Local news stations belong to one of a group of larger news stations called networks. Some of these networks include ABC, CBS, NBC, CNN, and Fox. These networks send reporters and videographers around the world to cover news as it happens, then send these reports and pictures by satellite to the local stations to use on their news shows. Sometimes the stations will show an entire report and other times they'll show only a few scenes from the event as the news anchor reads the accompanying information. This is called a voice-over.

Newspapers

Many television reporters can get good story ideas from reading the newspaper. A story from the newspaper can be even more interesting when shown on television because viewers can see and hear the event as it happens. For example, a newspaper story about a circus that is in town would make an exciting television news story . Seeing the elephants, lions, and tigers, as well as all the circus people setting up the circus, would be really bring this story to life.

Police Radio

Television news is exciting when it can report the news as it is happening. Every news station has a police radio in the newsroom so the staff can hear when a police officer is sent to the scene of a crime or accident. Then the news station can immediately send an ENG team to cover the story. The team may even report "live" from the scene if the event is important to the community.

Telephones

The telephone provides a quick way to check the accuracy of news stories. A reporter can easily call and go over the facts and events that have occurred before leaving the newsroom. Car phones have recently made this news source even more available. Reporters can be checking out news facts as they are driving to the scene.

News Beats

There are some places in the community where news events happen every day. These places may include the city hall, police station, courthouse, or even school district offices. Reporters often are assigned to check these areas for news stories each day. This daily coverage is called a news beat. Although these locations do not always supply the day's "top stories," they do provide news and information for the people in the community.

Mail Handouts

Mail handouts are often called "press releases." They are sent to news stations by individuals or organizations seeking publicity for their event or activity. For example, if your club was having a "pet fair" to raise money for the local animal shelter, you would want to send a press release to your local news station in the hope that they would broadcast a report about it. News stations often assist clubs by reporting events that raise money to help others in the community.

News Bureaus

Many local news stations have offices and newsrooms located in neighboring cities so that they can cover stories in those areas. The news that happens there may be important enough to broadcast, but the city may be too far away to send a reporter every time an event occurs. For example, events from the state capital may be important to other cities in the state. These bureaus send their reports back to the main news station for broadcast each day.

Tips

Someone may call the station to supply information about a news story. This is called a "tip." Very often those persons who supply tips don't want anyone to know who they are because it would put them in a dangerous situation. They may lose their job or be hurt by someone who is angry that they gave information to the news station. Sometimes tips can help stop a crime, solve a crime, or prevent a bad situation from continuing.

Future Files

Most newsrooms have a file, or calendar, on which they record information about upcoming events. Reporters will check the future file each day to see if any of these events might make a good story for the daily newscast.

Stringers

"Stringers" are people who have their own video equipment and sell their stories to news stations. Sometimes there are so many events happening in one day in the community that the news station will hire a stringer to videotape one or two of the events.

As you can see, news stations depend upon many sources for their news. Good reporters use a lot of sources and ideas for reporting news stories. No matter what the story, however, a good reporter will carefully check all of the facts before going on the air.

NOTES:

ACTIVITY 9: WHERE DO THEY GET THE NEWS?

Fill in the blank with the correct news source.

Wire services	Telephones	Networks	Tips
News bureaus	Newspaper	Stringers	
Police radio	News beats	Mail handouts	

1. This news source sends out information from around the world to news stations.

   _____

2. Newsrooms listen to this throughout the day to find out information as it happens.

   _____

3. Reporters even have these in their cars so they can check out facts very quickly on the way to the story.

   _____

4. Local places in the community where reporters are sent each day to check on stories and events.

   _____

5. Read by reporters each day, this news source can give information about possible news stories.

   _____

6. Large news stations that cover events around the world and send reports and pictures to local news stations.

   _____

7. Information given by someone who does not want his or her name known.

   _____

8. People who work for themselves who sell news stories or videotaped events to local news stations.

   _____

9. Newsrooms and offices owned by the local news station but are located in neighboring cities.

   _____

10. Sometimes called "press releases," these news sources are mailed to news stations for publicity purposes.

    _____

NOTES:

CAREERS IN TELEVISION
LESSON 1
DIRECTOR WILLY DOBY

Willy Doby is the director for the morning and afternoon news at WCPX Channel 6 in Orlando, Florida. Each day Willy meets with his producer to discuss what topics will be shown on the news. Willy has to decide how things will happen during the show. He must know the order of news stories and videotapes, which camera will have each shot, and what kind of graphics will be used. As a director, it is Willy's job to make sure everyone on the crew knows what to do and when to do it.

How did Willy learn to become a director? He first became interested in photography and worked on his school newspaper and yearbook. He got his first job in television as a camera operator. He worked hard at his job and soon wanted to know even more about television news. Willy stayed late at night watching the directors working on the late night news. Soon he got his chance to become a director, too! Willy enjoys being in charge of the 10-15 people who work together each day to produce a newscast.

Being a director is an important job. You have to be able to watch and direct many people at a time. You have to make sure everyone knows what is going to happen at each moment of the news show. Willy's goal is to direct the newscast so that the people in the community not only watch the news, but enjoy it as well.

When Willy is not at work, he enjoys being with his three children. He loves to work around the house and the yard. Willy also enjoys playing racquetball.

From *Television Production for Elementary Schools*. © 1994 Keith Kyker and Christopher Curchy
Libraries Unlimited, Inc., Englewood, CO 1-800-237-6124

Activities

1. What are some of the things Willy Doby has to do as director of a news show?

2. As a director, Willy has to communicate with many crew members during the news broadcast. Make a list of the people you think the director would talk to during the broadcast of a news show.

3. Watch the ending credits of one of your local news show broadcasts. Who is the director?

CAREERS IN TELEVISION
LESSON 2
PRODUCER ASHLEY UDELL

Ashley Udell is a producer for the morning news at WCPX Channel 6 in Orlando, Florida. Each day Ashley must gather all the news that is to be on the morning edition of the news show. She uses many sources of information to help her decide how the information will be presented. Some stories will be covered by ENG reporters and shown on videotape. Other stories will be voice-overs—the news anchor will read the information as pictures are shown from videotape. Ashley also must write some of the news information and decide how graphics will be used during the show.

Ashley always wanted to be a writer. She went to the University of North Carolina and majored in journalism. While she was there she became interested in television production. Her favorite part of her job as producer is presenting the news as creatively as possible. One of the hardest parts of her job is fitting all the news each day into a 30-minute show.

When Ashley isn't working at Channel 6, she enjoys going to places where she can just watch and enjoy life. She likes to watch people going from place to place. She also enjoys reading about life and the world around us.

If you would like to be a producer some day, Ashley's advice is to write and learn about the world around you. Learn to write your thoughts in a clear manner and keep your facts straight.

Activities

1. What are some of the duties of a news show producer?

2. Pretend you are a news show producer. Look at one of your daily newspapers and select what stories you would put on your news show. Remember, you only have a 30-minute show, including commercials.

3. Watch a local news show. Make a list of the topics and stories that were reported on the show. Which ones were videotaped reports by ENG reporters, which ones were just voice-overs, and which ones only used a graphic as the anchor read the story?

From *Television Production for Elementary Schools.* © 1994 Keith Kyker and Christopher Curchy
Libraries Unlimited, Inc., Englewood, CO 1-800-237-6124

NOTES:

CAREERS IN TELEVISION
LESSON 3
NEWS ANCHOR MARY HAMILL

Mary Hamill is a news anchor on WCPX Channel 6 in Orlando, Florida. Each day thousands of people in central Florida watch and listen as Mary reports news on the evening and nightly editions of the news show. It takes a lot of preparation to get these newscasts ready. Mary gets up early each day to learn about what important events might be happening around the world. She reads the newspaper and listens to the radio to get additional information. She arrives at work three to four hours before the news broadcast to begin writing and putting together her stories.

Prior to the newscast, Mary meets with the producer and director to decide how the stories will be shown and what angle of each story will be featured. Being a news anchor often means working long hours and working late at night to make sure the news is accurate and interesting. Meeting deadlines is important in the newsroom, and Mary enjoys the satisfaction of getting her job done on time.

How did Mary Hamill get to be a news anchor? She went to college in Missouri and studied print journalism. She also loved acting in the theater! One day someone suggested she check out television broadcasting. Mary got involved in her college television program and found it fun and interesting. Her professional career began with an internship in a television news station.

When Mary is not at work, she enjoys reading, swimming, and spending time with her family.

Activities

1. What are some of the things Mary Hamill does to prepare for each day's news show?

2. Pretend you are a news anchor on a local news show. Take a newspaper story and rewrite it as a television news story. What video pictures would you want to show as you read it on the air?

From *Television Production for Elementary Schools.* © 1994 Keith Kyker and Christopher Curchy
Libraries Unlimited, Inc., Englewood, CO 1-800-237-6124

3. Who is your favorite local TV news anchor? Write him or her a letter telling about your program at school and request an autographed picture.

CAREERS IN TELEVISION
LESSON 4
WEATHER ANCHOR PAT MICHAELS

Pat Michaels is the weather anchor on WCPX Channel 6 in Orlando, Florida. The daily weather report is watched by many people in central Florida making plans to go to the beach, the theme parks, or simply to go to work. Pat Michaels spends a lot of time trying to make sure his weather report is correct each day.

Pat arrives at Channel 6 an hour before the morning news is broadcast. He reviews maps that are sent by satellite showing the latest weather information: temperatures, wind speed and direction, humidity, and barometer readings. He uses a computer to input all of this information on maps that are shown on his weather report. Pat does not write down what he is going to say for each report. From past experience, he can simply go on camera and give the weather based on the information he has on his maps and computer.

Pat did not know he was going to be a weather anchor when he was in school, but he did know he was interested in radio and television. He began doing radio broadcasts when he was only 15. His first work in television was doing voice-overs for commercials and television promos. While he was working at the television station, the weather anchor decided to leave for another job. The station's management asked Pat to be the new weather anchor, and he agreed. He learned a lot about being a weather anchor by being one! He also took some classes in meteorology so he would know more about weather and weather patterns.

When Pat is not at Channel 6 working on his weather forecasts, he enjoys going cycling. It's his favorite hobby, and he bicycles about one hour every day.

From *Television Production for Elementary Schools.* © 1994 Keith Kyker and Christopher Curchy
Libraries Unlimited, Inc., Englewood, CO 1-800-237-6124

Activities

1. What are some of the things Pat Michaels has to do to prepare each day's weather forecast?

2. Watch the weather forecast on your local news show. What information is given about the weather in your city?

3. What is a barometer? What is meant by a high or low air mass? Use an encyclopedia to find out!

4. Look up the weather forecast in your daily newspaper. Use it to make a weather forecast for your school news show.

CAREERS IN TELEVISION
LESSON 5
WRITER KATHY YAROSH

Kathy Yarosh is a writer at WCPX Channel 6 in Orlando, Florida. She not only writes commercials but produces them. Writing commercials is an interesting job. Kathy meets with the clients and talks with them about the kinds of commercials they need for their products. Kathy decides what each commercial needs to look like and what information about the product should be in the commercial. She is responsible for hiring the talent and for deciding where to shoot the commercial. She must also choose what kind of music and graphics to use in the commercial. One of the most difficult skills of being a good writer is using your creativity to make each commercial interesting and successful. One of Kathy's funniest commercials involved an actor dressed up in a gorilla suit jumping up and down on patio furniture to show how sturdy it really was!

How do you get to be a writer for television? Kathy was enrolled at the University of Central Florida and working as an intern at Channel 6 when she was offered a job. Kathy says that being very persistent and volunteering to do *any* job at a television station is one of the best ways to get a job in television. It worked for her!

Whenever Kathy isn't busy writing and producing commercials at Channel 6, she enjoys reading and doing crafts. Kathy is also a real science fiction fan and enjoys watching science fiction movies and television programs.

Activities

1. What are some of the things Kathy Yarosh must do before she begins videotaping her commercial?

2. What is your favorite commercial on television? What do you like about it?

3. Draw a picture of a make-believe product or invention. Now write a commercial about it. Videotape your commercial.

NOTES:

CAREERS IN TELEVISON
LESSON 6
AUDIO ENGINEER CHRIS FLORA

Sound is a very important part of television and movies. Chris Flora is the audio engineer at WCPX Channel 6 in Orlando, Florida. Chris runs the soundboard during the news show. He has to balance all of the sound used in the newscast, including all of the anchor microphones, sound from videotaped stories, music used in the news show, and sometimes sound from "live" reports. Chris also is responsible for providing sound for commercials, special reports, and station promos. He even helps edit sound effects for special projects.

Chris loves sound as a hobby, too. He even had his own sound studio in his house! He first became interested in television production when he saw how exciting it was to use sound with video. Putting music with pictures and stories was fun and challenging for him. After Chris finished two years of college, he decided to go to Full Sail Center for the Recording Arts to learn more about sound and audio techniques. This training was very helpful in getting his job at Channel 6.

Being an audio engineer for a television station can sometimes be a very hectic job. When a really big news event happens in the community, everyone at the station is working hard to bring the news as it happens. Chris must run sound from many sources at one time so reporters in the studio and reporters at the scene can report the news at the same time. He must concentrate on his job and mix the sound quickly and correctly in the middle of all of this excitement. For Chris it is very rewarding when the news show ends and he knows he did a good job on a difficult day.

Activities

1. As an audio engineer, Chris Flora has a lot of responsibilities. List some of the jobs he does each day.

2. Music is an important part of television. Watch your television for 30 minutes after school one day. Make a list of all of the shows,

From *Television Production for Elementary Schools.* © 1994 Keith Kyker and Christopher Curchy
Libraries Unlimited, Inc., Englewood, CO 1-800-237-6124

commercials, or television promos that use music. Did you recognize any of the songs?

3. Movie soundtracks are very popular. See how many students in your class buy tapes or CDs of movie soundtracks.

CAREERS IN TELEVISON
LESSON 7
VIDEOGRAPHER/EDITOR
DAVE TREIBER

Recording news events and stories on videotape is one of the most important jobs at a television station. Dave Treiber is a videographer at WCPX Channel 6 in Orlando, Florida. He also edits news reports that he has videotaped so they can be broadcast on the local news. Dave operates the studio cameras and also goes out on assignments with Channel 6 reporters.

When Dave is working with a reporter on a news story, he has many responsibilities. He has to make sure that he records the necessary camera shots to make an interesting and realistic report. Sound and lighting are also his responsibility. Dave even acts as a director on location.

After 15 years as a videographer, Dave has learned to work quickly and efficiently. A news videographer has to be able to record things as they happen. There is no second chance for a camera shot when you are videotaping live news stories. In news reporting, the story has to be ready before the news show begins. Making the deadline is important for ENG crews.

Dave enjoys being a videographer. He became interested in television and film when he was a little boy. He would go to the movies quite often and think about the camera work, lighting, and special effects as he watched the film. Dave went to college at the University of Central Florida and he also attended the American Film Institute to develop his camera skills. If you'd like to be a videographer some day, Dave's advice is to read as much as you can about cameras and camera techniques. And, of course, use a camera every time you get a chance!

Activities

1. What are some of the jobs Dave Treiber must do as a videographer at Channel 6?

2. Watch your local news show. What types of studio camera shots do they use? How many people are in each shot? How do they frame each shot? Do the cameras move while the shot is being broadcast?

3. Watch one of your favorite video movies. Did you see a great camera shot or special effect? Bring it in and share them with your class.

CAREERS IN TELEVISION
LESSON 8
ELECTRONIC GRAPHIC ARTIST
JULIE NORTHLAKE

An electronic graphic artist designs graphics, logos, and pictures used on television news shows. Julie Northlake is an electronic graphic artist at WCPX Channel 6 in Orlando, Florida. She designs the graphics used by Channel 6 in their news shows, commercials, and station promos. In the past, graphic artists used paint and brushes to create television graphics. Now, Julie uses computers to help her create graphics from pictures, printed material, or even scenes recorded on videotape.

Julie enjoys her work because every day offers her a different opportunity to design new and interesting graphics. Electronic graphics have become an important part of television news shows. Those pictures placed over the anchors' shoulders as they report the news are designed by a graphic artist. Julie even designs the maps used during traffic reports.

Julie first became interested in television production when she was attending Stevens College in Missouri. She was enrolled in the TV/Radio/Film program. Originally she wanted to be a writer. But after taking some art and photography classes, she became interested in television graphics. At that time, television graphics were made by first photographing the picture or graphic and then recording it on videotape. With the new computers, that method is no longer used in most television stations.

Julie enjoys spending time with her family when she is not working at Channel 6. She likes to exercise and runs to keep herself healthy. She says that internships are a good way to meet people and find a job in the television production field. She recommends showing people you are interested in learning more about television production by volunteering to help work in television stations and other production studios.

Activities

1. What are some of the ways an electronic graphic artist assists in producing a news show?

2. Watch your local news. Make a list of all of the kinds of graphics used during the show.

3. Logos are used by a lot of companies to identify their products. Many logos now appear on clothes, shoes, hats, and even toys. Make a collage for your classroom out of logos cut from newspapers and magazines.

4. Design a neat logo for your school news show.

OBJECT LESSON 1
"WHAT ARE SOUND WAVES, ANYWAY?"
HOW MICROPHONES WORK

Clap your hands! Did you hear the sound as your hands came together? Of course you did, but do you know how the sound traveled from your hands to your ear?

Sound is really a vibration that travels through the air. The vibration is called a sound wave. Sound waves travel through the air just like water waves travel through the ocean. When you clapped your hands together, they made a vibration in the air. This vibration created a sound wave that traveled through the air into your ear. Sound waves can travel through air, water, and even solid objects like doors and desks.

Place your ear on a table or desk. Tap a pencil on the top of the desk. Did you hear the sound as it traveled through the desk? Try tapping the pencil on the sides or legs of the table or desk. Can you still hear the sound?

Let's try and see what sound waves look like as they reach your ear or a microphone. Fill a large shallow pan with water. Place a glass on its side in the water. Place the open end of the glass so it is facing the center of the pan.

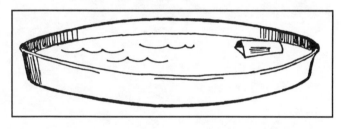

Now drop a small object (a penny, rock, marble) into the center of the pan. Do you see how the object caused a vibration in the water? Watch how this vibration makes waves that travel from the source of the vibration into the glass. This shows us how sound waves can travel through the air into your microphone. The microphone, like the glass, receives the sound waves. Then the microphone changes these sound waves into electrical energy and records them on your videotape.

Other Activities

1. Using an encyclopedia or science reference book, find out how fast sound travels.

2. Read about the invention of the telephone or telegraph.

3. Make a tin-can telephone. Try using different materials (string, fishing line, wire, rope) for the connecting wires. Which one works best? Why?

From *Television Production for Elementary Schools.* © 1994 Keith Kyker and Christopher Curchy
Libraries Unlimited, Inc., Englewood, CO 1-800-237-6124

NOTES:

OBJECT LESSON 2
"HOW DOES THE BIG WORLD FIT IN THAT LITTLE LENS?"
HOW A LENS GATHERS AND FOCUSES LIGHT

The lens of a camera looks so small, yet it can be used to record very large scenes. Sometimes we use the camera to get a good close-up view of a person or object. The size of the lens does not change, but the size of the recorded picture certainly does! How does a video camera do this?

Most video cameras have a zoom lens. This is a lens that can move to change the size of the scene you are videotaping. You can change the scene from a close-up (telephoto) shot to a wide-angle shot by using the zoom control on the camera. When you zoom in for a close-up, the camera lens is really moving farther away from the CCD chip, which is the device that changes light into electricity. This distance is measured in millimeters. As the distance gets larger, so does the view of your object. When you zoom out for a wide-angle shot, the lens moves closer to the CCD chip.

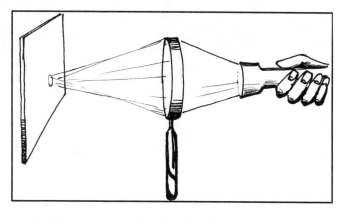

Let's see how these distances affect the size of the recorded images and scenes. You will need a magnifying glass, a flashlight, and a piece of dark cardboard or construction paper. Hold the magnifying glass about 6 inches in front of the flashlight. Shine the light through the magnifying glass onto the construction paper. Look at the size and shape of the circle of light on the paper.

Now move the magnifying glass farther away from the flashlight. What happens to the circle of light on the paper? What happens as you move the magnifying glass farther and farther away from the flashlight? Start moving the magnifying glass closer to the flashlight. What begins to happen to the circle of light?

Changing the distances between the light source (flashlight) and the lens (magnifying glass) changes the image on the piece of paper. When you zoom in and out on your video camera, you are also changing the distance between the lens and the imaging source. This is the reason your recorded pictures can be very large (close-ups) or very small (wide-angle).

Other Activities

1. Read about lenses in the encyclopedia. Look up the differences between concave and convex lenses.

2. A microscope can also change the size of an image by changing distances between the lens and the object viewed. Use a microscope to view a piece of onion skin. What happens as the lens moves farther from the object?

3. Bring a pair of binoculars to class. Look through them. Now turn them around and look through the other end (large side). What is different? Why?

OBJECT LESSON 3
"HOW DO THOSE THREE SKINNY LEGS HOLD UP THAT HEAVY CAMERA?"
HOW A TRIPOD WORKS

You have probably seen a camera set up on a tripod. Did you ever wonder how a support with such skinny legs could hold up that heavy camera? Well, it's really a matter of balance!

A tripod is designed with three legs connected at the top by a camera base, called the tripod head. When the camera is placed on the tripod head, its weight is equally distributed to each tripod leg. That means that each leg is only supporting one-third of the camera weight. When the tripod's legs are spread apart, the camera is balanced between them. This provides a steady platform for the video camera. A tripod can support objects that weigh much more than it does because it uses balance and weight distribution to assist in supporting the video camera.

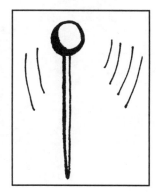

Let's try making our own tripods to see how balance works in supporting objects. You will need some clay (plasticene, play-doh, salt-dough, or molding clay) and three toothpicks (coffee stirrers, straws, wooden dowels). Make a ball (about 1 inch in diameter) out of the clay. Stick one of the toothpicks into the center of the clay. Can you get your clay to stand up on the end of the toothpick?

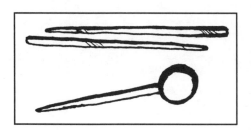

Now try sticking two toothpicks into the center of the clay. Will it stand up?

How about three toothpicks? Will your clay be able to stand up now?

How large a ball can your "tripod" support? Experiment with larger and larger balls of clay. Perhaps you can even use a scale to weigh the balls of clay to see how much weight your toothpick tripod will support. I'll bet you'll be surprised at the strength of these three skinny legs!

From *Television Production for Elementary Schools.* © 1994 Keith Kyker and Christopher Curchy
Libraries Unlimited, Inc., Englewood, CO 1-800-237-6124

Other Activities

1. How much do tripods cost? Are there different kinds of tripods? Obtain a catalog from a local or national tripod retailer (Bogen, Sanford Davis, etc.) and look at the various kinds of tripods and their costs.

2. What do you call a camera support with only one leg? Can you find one in a store or catalog? How would it be used?

3. What do television stations use to hold their large video cameras? Visit a local station and ask to see their camera supports.

OBJECT LESSON 4
"WHY IS THAT MAN POINTING A SALAD BOWL AT THOSE FOOTBALL PLAYERS?" HOW A PARABOLIC DISH MICROPHONE WORKS

Have you ever gone to a football game, or watched one on TV, and saw a person holding a round dish-shaped object on the sidelines? The person walked along the sidelines following the action on the field and aiming the center of the dish at the players. But this is no ordinary dish. This dish is really a special kind of microphone called a parabolic dish microphone. The

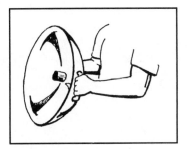

microphone is held in the center of the dish. It is used to record the sounds of the football game coming from the field. In baseball, a parabolic dish microphone is used to record the sound of the ball hitting a catcher's glove, or even a bat! The parabolic dish surrounding the microphone helps the microphone to hear better! The sides of the dish reflect the sound waves into the microphone. A bigger dish can reflect more sound than a smaller dish.

Cup one of your hands to your ear. Listen as a friend talks, whistles, or rings a bell. How does it sound? Now remove your hand. Hear the difference? Your hand is helping to reflect the sound waves into your ear. Does size make a difference? Let's find out!

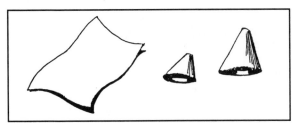

Make some "cones" out of construction paper. They should be different sizes.

Have a friend ring a bell or make a sound from across the room. Hold one of the smallest cones up to your ear. How does the sound change? Why?

Now hold the largest cone to your ear. Is there a difference in sound? Why?

Try and see how far away the sound can be before you cannot hear it anymore!

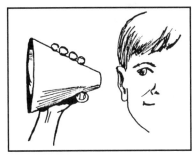

Other Activities

1. Ask a local television station to bring a dish microphone to your class and demonstrate how it works.

2. Read about animals and how they use their ears for hunting and protection. Why do rabbits have such big ears? How about the rabbit fox?

GLOSSARY

adapter. A device used to achieve compatibility between two items of audiovisual equipment.

aperture. The opening of the lens, as controlled by the iris.

aspect ratio. The relationship of the height of a television picture to its width. The aspect ratio for television is 3 x 4, meaning that the television screen is three units tall and four units wide.

assemble editing. The process of television postproduction that involves duplicating the audio and video while creating a new control track.

audio dub. An editing technique that involves erasing the existing audio track on a videotape and replacing it with a new audio track.

audio mixer. An electronic component that facilitates the selection and combination of audio signals.

audio/video mixer. A single electronic component that consists of an audio mixer and a video mixer, switcher, or special effects generator. Also called an A/V mixer.

automatic focus. A feature on most consumer and industrial video cameras and camcorders that automatically makes minor focal length adjustments, thus eliminating the need to manually focus the camera. Also referred to as autofocus.

automatic gain control. A feature on most video cameras and camcorders that, when engaged, boosts the signal to its optimum output level. Automatic gain control (AGC) is available for video, and less frequently for audio use.

automatic iris. A feature on most video cameras and camcorders that automatically creates the lens aperture that allows the imaging device to perform under optimum conditions.

backlight. (1) A lighting instrument placed between the talent and the backdrop to eliminate shadows produced by other lighting instruments and create the illusion of depth; (2) a feature on some consumer camcorders that boosts the video signal to compensate for poorly lit talent standing in front of very bright backgrounds.

Beta. A videocassette format that uses ½-inch wide videotape.

BNC. A video connector characterized by a single shaft enclosed by a twist-lock mechanism.

box house. A slang term for a mail-order business for audio and video components. Box houses frequently offer little or no consumer support or equipment repair.

camcorder. An item of video equipment used to create and record the video signal that consists of a video camera permanently attached to a video deck.

cardioid. Another name for the unidirectional microphone pickup pattern. The name *cardioid* comes from the heart shape of the pickup pattern. The terms *super-cardioid*, *hyper-cardioid*, and *ultra-cardioid* describe more narrow pickup patterns. (*See* **unidirectional**.)

CCD. *See* charge-coupled device

character generator. A video component that allows the typing of words and simple graphics onto the television screen.

charge-coupled device (CCD). An imaging device used in most video cameras and camcorders.

close-up. A video shot consisting of the head and shoulders of the subject.

condenser microphone. A microphone that contains an element made of two small vibrating magnetized plates.

contrast ratio. The comparison of the brightest part of the screen to the darkest part of the screen, expressed as a ratio. The maximum contrast ratio for television production is 30 x 1.

crawl. Graphics that move across the bottom of the television screen, usually from right to left. A "weather alert" that moves along the bottom of the screen is a crawl.

deck-to-deck editing. The process of postproduction that involves combining video and audio by connecting two VCRs or video decks together, without the benefit of an editing control unit.

digital zoom. A feature found on some consumer camcorders that electronically increases the lens zoom capability by selecting the center of the image and enlarging it digitally.

dissolve. A video transition in which the first video signal is gradually replaced by the second video signal.

dolly. (n.) A set of casters attached to the legs of a tripod to allow the tripod to roll.

dolly. (v.) A forward/backward rolling movement of the camera on top of the tripod dolly.

dynamic microphone. A microphone containing an element that consists of a diaphragm and moving coil.

ECU. *See* **editing control unit**

editing. The process of combining, adding, and deleting audio and video elements to create a video program.

editing control unit (ECU). A microprocessor that controls two or more video decks or VCRs and facilitates frame-accurate editing.

ENG. Electronic news gathering.

establishing shot. A long camera angle that shows enough of the environment to orient the viewer to the program's setting.

F-connector. a video connector characterized by a single metal wire. F-connectors may be either push-on or screw-post types.

---

fade. A video technique in which the picture is gradually replaced with a background color.

fader bar. A vertical slide controller on audio and video equipment.

fill light. A lighting instrument used to illuminate the part of the subject not adequately illuminated by the key light.

flying head. A video head that engages when the video deck is on "pause," providing a clear still-frame image.

focal length. The distance from the optical center of the lens to the front of the imaging device, measured in millimeters.

font. A style of type. Many character generators offer the user a menu of several fonts.

gain. An increase in the output of the audio or video signal.

gel. A sheet of thin, plasticlike translucent material placed over a lighting instrument to change the color or diffusion of the light.

head. A magnet used to record or play a signal on a magnetic medium, like videotape.

headroom. (1) The composition technique of allowing a small but comfortable area above the head of the subject; (2) the area between the top of the subject's head and the top of the television screen.

Hi-8. A high-quality videotape format that consists of magnetic tape 8 millimeters wide in a small plastic videocassette shell.

high-speed shutter. A feature on video cameras and camcorders that allows detail enhancement of fast-moving objects by electronically dividing the CCD into imaging sections.

imaging device. The part of the video camera or camcorder that converts light into an electrical signal.

impedance. A resistance to signal flow. Microphones and audio mixers are rated for impedance.

insert editing. The process of television postproduction that combines audio and video signals on an existing control track.

iris. The mechanism that controls the lens aperture.

jog. Frame-by-frame advancement of a videotape in a VCR or video deck.

jog-shuttle wheel. A dial on many video decks, VCRs, and editing control units that controls jog and shuttle functions.

key light. The lighting instrument that illuminates the subject.

lavaliere microphone. A small condenser microphone used in television production.

leadroom. (1) The composition technique of putting more space in front of a moving object than behind it; (2) the area between the front of a moving object and the side of the television screen.

lens. The curved glass on a video camera or camcorder that collects light.

macro lens. A lens used for videography when the camera-to-object distance is less than 2 feet. The macro lens is usually installed within the zoom lens of the video camera or camcorder.

microphone. An audio component that converts sound waves into electrical energy.

monitor. (1) A speaker or headphone set; (2) a video screen. A video monitor accepts a video signal and does not have a tuner.

monochrome. A video picture consisting of different saturations of a single color, usually gray; the technical term for black-and-white television.

monopod. A one-legged mounting support that helps the videographer steady the video camera or camcorder.

noseroom. (1) The composition technique that puts space between the nose of a subject in profile and the side of the television screen; (2) the area between the subject in profile and the side of the television screen.

omnidirectional. A microphone pickup pattern in which the microphone hears equally well from all sides.

$\frac{1}{8}$-inch mini. A small audio connector used frequently in consumer electronics.

$\frac{1}{4}$-inch phone. A connector used in audio production that is characterized by its single shaft with locking tip.

over-the-shoulder shot. A technique of video composition in which the shoulder and part of the back of the head of a worker, observer, or interview participant is included in the shot.

pan. A horizontal movement of a camera on top of a tripod.

phono (RCA). A connector used in audio and video components, characterized by its single-connection post and metal flanges.

pickup pattern. The description of the directionality of a microphone. The two prominent microphone pickup patterns are omnidirectional and unidirectional.

pixel. A single section of a CCD, capable of distinguishing chrominance (color) and luminance (brightness); professional slang for "picture element."

postproduction. The phase of television production that includes all activity after the raw footage is shot.

preproduction. The phase of television production that includes all activity before the raw footage is shot.

pressure zone microphone (PZM). A microphone consisting of a metal plate and a small microphone element. The PZM collects and processes all sound waves that strike the metal plate.

production. The phase of television production that includes recording the scenes of the program on videotape (shooting raw footage).

professional/industrial. The grade of audio and video equipment that falls between consumer (low end) and broadcast quality. Professional/industrial equipment is characterized by its durability, serviceability, and more professional end result.

PZM. *See* **pressure zone microphone**

raw footage. The unedited video and audio recorded during the production process.

RCA. *See* **phono (RCA)**

record review. A feature on many video cameras and camcorders that allows the videographer to see the last few seconds of video recorded on the videotape.

RF signal. The modulated composite (video and audio) signal produced by television stations and VCRs, and processed by televisions.

rule of thirds. The technique of video composition that draws an imaginary tic-tac-toe grid on the screen and places the most interesting/important parts of the scene along the lines and at their intersections.

S-VHS. A video format that uses VHS-sized cassettes and ½-inch S-VHS tape, to produce a signal with more than 400 lines of resolution. S-VHS is not just high-quality VHS. The S-VHS signal cannot be recorded on a VHS tape or recorded or played on a VHS VCR.

scrim. Translucent material made of cotton, spun glass, or synthetic material that is placed over a lighting instrument to reduce and/or diffuse its output.

scroll. Graphics that roll from the bottom to the top of the screen, for example, end credits.

shotgun microphone. A microphone with an extremely directional pickup pattern.

shuttle. A variable-rate search, forward or reverse, of a videotape using a video deck or VCR capable of such an operation.

special effects generator. A video component that processes the video signal and has the ability to manipulate the signal with a variety of wipes and distortions.

storyboard. (n.) A plan for a video project that consists of sketches of the desired shots and a description of the audio portion; (v.) the act of preparing a storyboard.

surface-mount microphone. A microphone with a flat back designed to be mounted on a flat surface, such as a conference table or the lid of a grand piano.

switcher. A video component that allows the selection of a video source from several sources input into the switcher. Most switchers allow the technician to perform wipes, dissolves, and fades.

TBC. *See* **time-base corrector**

telephoto lens. A long focal-length lens that allows videography from a great distance.

television. A combination tuner, RF modulator, picture tube, and audio speaker that converts the RF signal into picture and sound.

tilt. A horizontal movement of a video camera or camcorder on top of a tripod.

time-base corrector (TBC). A video component that digitizes inherently unstable video signals and converts them into rock-solid video. A TBC usually has controls for manipulating the output signal's color, brightness, and strength.

tracking. The video control that allows proper placement of the videotape across the video and audio heads.

treatment. A one- to-two page description of a video project.

trigger. A slang term for the button on the video camera or camcorder that, when depressed, sends a signal to the videotape recorder to begin or stop recording.

tripod. A three-legged video camera or camcorder mounting device that provides steady, tireless service.

tripod dolly. A combination tripod and dolly.

unidirectional. A microphone pickup pattern in which the microphone processes most of its signal from sound collected in front of the microphone, and very little from the sides and back of the microphone.

VCR. *See* **videocassette recorder**

vendor. A person or business that sells audio and/or video equipment.

VHS. A videocassette format characterized by a plastic shell and half-inch-wide videotape. VHS is an abbreviation for "video home system" as created by the JVC company. VHS is the dominant format for consumer-oriented video equipment and videotape.

VHS-C. A videocassette format characterized by a plastic shell and half-inch-wide videotape. VHS-C-recorded tape is compatible with VHS if an adapter is used. VHS-C was developed as a way to create a VHS signal with a smaller videocassette, thus using a small camcorder.

video camera. A video component consisting of a lens, a viewfinder, and at least one imaging device that converts light into an electrical video signal.

video noise. A poor-quality video signal within the standard video signal. Also called "snow" (slang).

video signal. The electrical signal produced by video components.

videocassette. A length of videotape wound around two reels and enclosed in a plastic shell.

videocassette recorder (VCR). An electronic component consisting of a tuner, an RF modulator, and a video deck used for recording and playback of a videocassette.

video deck. An electronic component consisting of a video/audio head assembly, a system of transporting a videotape past the heads, and operational controls, used for recording and playback of videotape.

videographer. A person who operates a video camera or camcorder.

videography. Operation of a video camera or camcorder in video production.

videotape. A thin strip of plastic material containing metal particles that are capable of recording and storing a magnetic charge.

viewfinder. A small monochrome monitor mounted on a video camera or camcorder.

volume unit (VU) meter. A device used for measuring the intensity of an audio signal.

VU. *See* **volume unit meter**

white balance. (n.) The control on a video camera or camcorder that allows the videographer to make minor adjustments in the color output of the camera; (v.) the process of adjusting the video camera or camcorder's color response to the surrounding light.

wide-angle lens. A lens with a very short focal length used for gathering light from a wide vista at a close distance.

wipe. A video transition is which one video source replaces another with a distinct line or lines of definition.

wireless microphone system. A microphone system consisting of a microphone, an FM transmitter, and a tuned receiving station that eliminates the need for long runs of microphone cable.

XLR. An audio connector characterized by three prongs covered by a metal sheath.

zoom lens. A lens with a variable focal length.

INDEX